# ALSO BY BYRON TULLY

Old Money Style: The Gentleman's Edition

❖

Old Money, New Woman: How To Manage Your Money &
Your Life

❖

The Hindu Way To Wealth - My Private Coversations with
One of India's Richest Men

❖

The Old Money Money Guide To Marriage:
Getting It Right - Making It Last

# The
# Hindu Way
# To
# Wealth

# The Hindu Way To Wealth

My Private Coversations with One
of India's Richest Men

BYRON TULLY

THE HINDU WAY TO WEALTH

Copyright 2020 by Byron Tully

First edition printed in 2013

*Edited by Weatherford Bradley*
*Copyright 2020 | All rights reserved.*
*Cover and book design by Kedi Darby*

*"India is the cradle of the human race, the birth-place of human speech, the mother of history, the grandmother of legend, and the great grandmother of tradition. Our most valuable and most instructive materials in the history of man are treasured up in India only."*

- Mark Twain

# CONTENTS

# INTRODUCTION

It didn't exactly start off well. I was scheduled to meet with Mahesh (not his real name) at the Ritz Carlton Hotel in downtown Los Angeles on a rainy Wednesday morning. The hotel was only twenty minutes from where I was staying, and I arrived early. His assistant met me in the lobby and delicately informed me that the lunch we had scheduled was, in all likelihood, not going to happen. Perhaps Mahesh would be available for coffee...? Her voice spun up an octave at the end of the sentence.

Was she asking me? Or just wandering out loud? I'd skipped breakfast, anticipating a world-class lunch in the company of one of India's most successful businessmen. This was a letdown. A friend of a friend had sent me a text the week before. The mode of communication being what it is, the details were vague, but the following phone conversation was not: the multimillionaire (perhaps billionaire, for all I knew) had read "The Old Money Book" and wanted to meet me, the author.

It was both flattering and puzzling. Why would he want to meet me? The book was selling well, but it was hardly Harry Potter. I wasn't that famous, and, by his standards, certainly not that rich. I surmised he didn't want to have a *selfie* taken with me to post on Instagram or want my autograph in his copy of "The Old Money Book". He didn't have a new venture that he wanted me to invest in, I was certain. And I'd known rich people who like to hang out with writers, singers, and artists so they can be cool. Everyone who knows me knows I don't have the patience for that. The first "friend" in the "friend of a friend" equation would never have roped me into a situation like that.

So what did he want? I asked the friend of a friend on the phone, as diplomatically as possible, putting a pin in the not infrequent request to be introduced to people I know in the entertainment industry. The answer was slightly a relief, but no more enlightening. "Oh, no, he doesn't care for actors. He just liked your book and wants to meet with you. He's social that way, curious."

'Curious' was the word for the day, to be sure. I was on a deadline with another book, had a meeting the next day about a script, and I wanted to be working and prepared. Instead, I was sitting in the Ritz Carlton, hungry as a bear, trying to get a straight answer from a pretty but slightly embarrassed assistant. Then, her phone chimed.

"Oh, he'll see you." And up we went. We entered the suite on the 25th floor. I'd been in a few luxurious hotel suites around the world, and this was definitely one of them. A financial news program murmured from the television, and a man's voice echoed around the corner: obviously a phone conversation was in progress. The assistant paused, and I paused. She waited. I waited. We waited.

A very ordinary looking Indian man puttered into view in an expensive shirt, linen pants, and bare feet. Phone to his ear, he nodded to his assistant and then waved to me pleasantly. I smiled and waved back. The conversation concluded with a smattering of English and Hindi, and he introduced himself with a firm, almost eager handshake.

"Please come in," he waved me forward to a sofa near a rain-soaked window. "Let's get some coffee to start and then order up some sandwiches. Grilled vegetable...?" The last part of the sentence went with a look to his assistant. She disappeared with a quick, "Yes, sir," and within seconds was speaking to someone in room service. Her tone was not casual: it was imperative. She needed a pot of fresh-brewed coffee and a plate of sandwiches, immediately. Apparently, the person on the other end of the phone asked what kind of sandwiches she preferred. Her response was a memorable, "We want all the sandwiches."

I smirked as a vision of every piece of bread, meat, vegetable, and cheese in the entire Ritz Carlton Hotel being slapped together, loaded onto a cart, and brought in to the suite *post haste* for our review and consumption. But I pulled focus and waited for the other shoe to drop.

"I read 'The Old Money Book'", said Mahesh after a minute or so of cordial chit-chat.

"Carol told me," I responded. "I hope you enjoyed it."

"Some of it I did enjoy, but some of it was non-sense."

I thought I might have misheard the last part of his statement. His accent was thick at times, but, no, his even gaze told me, that's what he said. "But that's okay. The book is selling, right?"

"It is selling." I was now thinking about grabbing a quick pizza somewhere, because this was going nowhere fast. I don't make a habit of following insults with inquiries, so I just sat there in silence.

The coffee promptly arrived on a cart. The assistant poured. I added sugar. Mahesh added cream. We sipped. Still, neither of us said a word. I had experienced this kind of behavior before, most often from bullies. If you felt compelled to fill the void with idle chatter, you showed weakness and found yourself at a disadvantage from that point forward. I felt no such compulsion. My host was no fool, and he wanted something, so he extended an olive branch.

"Maybe it's a cultural difference."

"In what way?"

"In your book, you emphasize keeping a low profile, living quietly, not letting anyone know you have money..."

"You're not exactly on the cover of Forbes," I replied. I'd done a 2-minute Google search for the *wealthiest men in India*, and Mahesh was nowhere to be found. Nevertheless, the second friend in the "friend of a friend" equation had rattled off a laundry list of the man's holdings and, even as a novice about the subcontinent's finance and business landscape, I recognized several of the companies mentioned. Then there were his international interests. By the time the friend ran out of breath, I had run out of doubt: the man was very, very wealthy.

"I don't care one way or the other," he shrugged. "But why do you advise people to live cheaply? That just doesn't make sense to me."

"Not everybody has your resources."

"But it's not like there's only so much money in the world." This was the first comment he made—and there would be many others over the course of our conversations—that made me hesitate and think. But I'd chew it over later.

"Americans have just had a history of consumerism and personal debt. They've made good money throughout their careers, but then they don't have anything to show for it at the end. That's why I wrote the book, and I think it helps address the problem."

"The credit card debt," he added, shaking his head.

"Yes."

"That's bad. That's like a disease."

"It is."

We'd worked our way around from the "nonsense" comment onto some firmer common ground when the news commentator on the television mentioned the price of gold. Mahesh's eyes cut to the set. He listened intently, almost without breathing, and then turned back to me.

"Would you like some more coffee?" he asked, then added, "We're going to have some sandwiches," before I could answer. No, I thought to myself, *we're going to have all the sandwiches*. Then, his cell phone dinged. He looked at it, read an email, and then turned back to me.

"Debt is bad. Working hard is good. Family is good." It was like he was reciting a grocery list.

"Spending is bad," I added.

"No! Spending is good!" he shot back. "It's got to flow! Money's got to be busy, or happy, or at rest in a natural state."

"Money's got to be happy?"

"It does. It has to be working in investments, or buying beautiful things for people to enjoy. Make their lives richer. Make them richer." His eyes had shot back to the television screen now. Currency markets. The dollar was up. Mahesh grunted.

"That is a cultural difference," I suggested. "I don't think spending makes people richer."

He looked at me for a moment. Then he seemed to sense something. "Let's eat," he said. The very next second, a bell rang. The assistant instantly went to the door and opened it. It was room service. In came a cart full of sandwiches.

Through lunch, we talked about cricket, which I knew next to nothing about, and soccer, which I knew a little more about. Mahesh told me briefly about his family, his education in America, and his return to India. He didn't come across as a type-A, blistering Gordon Gekko. He was smart, to be sure, but an ease circumvented his ambition. Democratically, his assistant ate in the dining room with us, adding her comments to the conversation without fear of reprisal. She was smart and attractive, but there was no misunderstanding: she was his assistant, not his girlfriend or mistress. Her eyes fired with admiration as she spoke of his wife and children. It wasn't flattery. Mahesh had done well in business, it was clear. He had, it seemed, been a good family man, too.

Finally, a lull hit the conversation, and the assistant excused herself. This was it. I'd been here two hours, and it had been interesting. But the time had come to discuss the reason that I'd been invited. And I still had no idea what it was.

"You've got your view, the western view, of how to create wealth," said Mahesh, tiptoeing into the subject. "I said it was nonsense. It's not nonsense, and I apologize if I offended you."

"I'm a writer. I hear all kinds of comments."

"You're helping people. That's your intention."

"Yes."

"So why don't you write another book, with my point of view?"

This kind of comment usually falls under the category of "I've got a great idea for a movie," which I hear once a week. Invariably, the concept that immediately follows is not a great idea for a movie. Furthermore, the distance between a great idea for something and the end product is usually a couple of years of blood, sweat, and tears. And usually mine, if it's a writing project. So the offer didn't exactly excite me.

"I don't think I'm your guy," I said honestly. "But I can ask some writers I know. They might jump at the chance."

"I'm not going to hire somebody," said Mahesh bluntly. "I don't want somebody that can be hired. I have certain beliefs. They've worked for me, obviously. But I want someone who can see the value in what I'm saying."

"I probably disagree with a lot of what you'd be saying."

"There's no believer like a convert." Then Mahesh laughed a laugh that I would hear many times afterward. It resonated with a child's pure wonder, joy, and amusement at the beauty and irony of life. And I laughed right along with him: if you think I'm ever going to equate spending money with becoming rich, I thought to myself, well...that is funny.

Our meeting concluded with me telling Mahesh that I'd think about it, a euphemism that generally translates to, "No, thank you."

Two days later, I had lunch with a friend who was in Los Angeles, visiting from Silicon Valley. I recounted my meeting with Mahesh, his philosophy of wealth and his interest in having me write about it.

"I think I met him at a wedding in San Jose," said my friend unexpectedly.

"Really?" I wasn't planning on writing for Mahesh, but I was definitely interested in getting another person's take on the man. "What was your impression?"

"Nice enough guy," shrugged my friend. "I didn't really talk with him, but the wedding was unbelievable."

"How's that?"

"They had Cirque de Soleil performing in a tent at the reception."

My response was expletive-laden and rhetorical.

My friend responded evenly, "No, I am not kidding you. They've got money, they spend it, but I don't think they're going to be running out anytime soon."

I sat there in shock: me, author of The Old Money Book, who preached economy in all things and most of all weddings, where the average American wasted (in my opinion) and average of $30,000 in 2013 on the ceremony instead of investing or saving that money for the future. This was a huge contradiction that left me shaking my head.

But my friend held an even look. His gaze told me that he wasn't finished with the bad news.

"What?" I asked, ready for the worst.

"Their philosophy..."

"Yeah?"

"I think there's something to it."

# THE GROUND RULES

I emailed Mahesh the next day and twelve hours later he emailed me back. Without much fanfare, we started to lay out the ground rules for our working relationship. He'd share his thoughts, beliefs, ideas, and anecdotes with me. I'd construct them into a narrative, and then I'd forward the text to him for review at various points in time as we progressed.

His demands were fairly modest. His name would not be used. His photo would not be taken. References made to his family, businesses, and employees would be vague enough to render his identity impossible to determine by any reader. He would have no ownership interest in the manuscript. If an agent, publisher, or journalist wanted to speak with him about the book, they would be, in his memorable way of putting things, "L.O.S.", meaning "S.O.L." (Sorely Out of Luck, to be polite.) I would be the face of the project. His anonymity would be assured. This was non-negotiable. I agreed instantly. Only his personal assistant and his wife knew we would be working together.

My demands were straightforward: I'd have the final edit on the manuscript. I could paraphrase his comments in the interest of clarity. (His syntax, vocabulary, and sometimes hysterically funny misuse of English phrases drove me to distraction, even in our initial meeting.) But if he had an issue with my wording, we could revisit the language and work out a compromise so that we both felt the concept in question had been expressed correctly. For example, if he referred to 'rupees', I could use 'dollars' in the text. But if there was a specific concept he felt wasn't being presented accurately, he could insist we go word for word in articulating it.

I would get a dozen meetings with him of at least one hour each within the subsequent three months (a huge time demand that I initially thought he would never honor, but did, even though times and dates were constantly rescheduled.) We'd email and talk on the phone at least twice a week. At any point in time, if I felt like he wasn't giving me the quantity or quality of material to would make a worthwhile book, I could scrap the project. If the project didn't go forward with me, he could enlist another writer, but only if I was compensated for my time.

I did not ask for or accept any upfront money, as I wanted to be free to write my book that expressed his philosophy. I wasn't going to be another employee, and I think he was secretly grateful: he knew nothing about writing and was happy to have proven expertise at an independent arm's length. I think he also liked the fact that I wasn't just another person looking for a paycheck. (As I spent time with him, I saw the relentless demands on his time, attention, and resources. It would have overwhelmed a lesser person, and my admiration for his patience and grace under pressure grew in the process. I also saw his uncanny ability to read people and situations instantly and accurately, responding honestly with rock-solid logic and sometimes razor-sharp language.)

During the time we worked together, I found a surprisingly circumspect, well-read, and very philosophical person behind Mahesh's business personae. His background, upon which I'm not at liberty to elaborate, exposed him to a wide range of literature, schools of thought, and experiences than what one would never expect a businessman to possess. Sometimes his conversation could sound as elevated as a mystic holding forth on a mountain top. Sometimes it hit street level—or below—when a subject irritated him. Sophisticated at times but often simple, soaked in spirituality, but candidly and fully human, contradictory but never dull: that was conversation with Mahesh.

In one of the initial conversations we had at the start of our time together, I asked him what he expected when the book was published, his answer was quick and unequivocal: "I don't want anything. Let's just get these ideas out there to people."

We that simple directive, we began.

# ABOUT HINDUISM

An enormous amount has been written about Hinduism over the centuries, and even more resources exist now online. So to write anything remotely approaching a definitive or exhaustive summary of it is impossible. Certainly, this book will only deal with one man's perspective on one aspect of Hinduism, so there is an ocean between reading this book and even remotely "understanding Hinduism". Nevertheless, I think it would be helpful to provide a brief overview of the history and fundamental concepts that Hindus seem to generally acknowledge and agree upon.

Hinduism, widely considered the world's oldest religion, originated in India sometime in the ancient past. About eighty percent of the people of India identify themselves as Hindu. About fifteen percent consider themselves Muslims. Christianity, Buddhism, and Sikhism have minor followings in the country.

Some consider Hinduism a religion; some consider it a philosophy; some consider it a way of life. And to some, it is all three. It is most accurately referred to as a tradition. Whatever label it's given, there are cautionary aspects about it that are wise to know and remember. Unlike Christianity or Buddhism, Hinduism has no founder. It does have sacred texts, the Vedas, but they are so old that nobody knows who wrote them or where they originated.

Many Westerners believe that Hinduism has many gods. In truth, it has only one, but Hindus worship a myriad of manifestations of that one god, the Supreme Being. Like other religions, Hinduism has temples, festivals, rituals, holidays, mythology, and saints. Practices and theology vary widely under its broad, welcoming umbrella.

And like other religions, there are adherents to Hinduism who make practical and inspired use of its rituals, traditions, and instructions and to lead productive and fulfilling lives. There are also the extremists, who use religion to justify prejudice, oppression, and violence, as we see happen all over the world, all the time, with all religions.

The four tenets of Hinduism are generally acknowledged to be the following:

- Dharma, which refers to duty or righteous living;

- Kama, which refers to earthly pleasures;

- Artha, which refers to the acquisition of wealth; and

- Moksha, which refers to the liberation of the soul from the cycle of birth, death, and rebirth on this earth.

The most important of these is moksha. To succinctly, if provincially, summarize moksha, one could say this: if it's true that you have to keep doing it (life) over and over again until you get it right, moksha is finally getting it right.

This belief in reincarnation, as well as the concept of karma (what goes around comes around), are the two concepts in Hinduism most familiar to Westerners. Westerners are also familiar with the physical practice of yoga and the spiritual practice of meditation.

Hinduism also offers four paths to reach the divine, to become one with God, or to realize your full spiritual and earthly potential, however you'd like to say it. These four paths are options which a devotee can choose, depending on their inclination and personality type. Again, Hinduism does not advocate one particular path to reach the goal of enlightenment or to obtain the feeling that you're living a worthwhile life. The path depends on the person, and most devotees seem to follow their own personal mix of the four paths.

The paths that a person can choose are as follows:

⚜ Bahkti Yoga, which is the path of devotion, in which the devotee worships, adores, and offers selfless service to a personal God (and the world) as a way to reach the divine, for those who lead with their heart;

⚜ Karma Yoga is the path of action, for persons who want to have their work be their worship and let their rewards belong to God, not to themselves, ideal for those "Type A" personalities like entrepreneurs;

⚜ Jnana Yoga is the path of wisdom and philosophical study, for those who are of an intellectual and literary bent; and

⚜ Raja Yoga, the path of physical mastery and meditation, for those who identify primarily with their bodies, like athletes, and for those whom meditation offers peace of mind and a window to the Infinite.

The personality descriptions that I've associated with each path above are solely based on my personal observations of people I've known who practice Hinduism and the paths they seem to gravitate toward. But, it should be stated that, spiritually speaking, everybody is really on their own path, regardless of their faith and the way they chose to approach it.

There are numerous misconceptions about Hindus and Hinduism. To eliminate these misunderstandings and have a greater understanding and appreciation of all religions, I recommend reading Huston Smith's "The World's Religions". This book articulates the fundamental teachings and traditions of numerous faiths, Hinduism included, in straightforward and easy-to-understand language. It also helps the reader to see how much all religions have in common, something that we all need to be reminded of on a regular basis.

# HINDUISM AND WEALTH

One aspect of Hinduism that has received less attention is its philosophy concerning wealth. Many religious leaders, past and present, have promoted the concept that money is the root of all evil. In fact, the scripture in the Bible reads, "The love of money is the root of all evil." There is a big difference.

Hinduism addresses this difference with its concept of detachment. Simply put, this means that you are free to acquire and enjoy material possessions, but you can't be attached to them. You can't let your happiness or your sense of self-worth depend on them. If you lose everything tomorrow, in terms of material possessions, you've got to be detached, shrug it off, and be as happy as you were the day before. Because, Hinduism teaches, only God is permanent. Everything else comes and goes. Get attached to money, fame, material possessions, or status, and you're going to suffer.

Hinduism is, if nothing else, practical, its elaborate rituals notwithstanding. It presents many of its teachings to people in down-to-earth terms, so they can live their day-to-day lives in a productive manner. Hinduism feels that if a person is impoverished or struggling with their physical needs, like putting food on the table, it is more difficult for them to give appropriate attention to their spiritual needs, like becoming one with God, or at least more God-like. It is also difficult for a rich person to be God-like if they're attached to worldly possessions. So everybody, rich and poor, has work to do: acquire wealth to take care of your family in this world, but practice detachment so you can keep your spiritual life in balance.

Hinduism also categorizes its teachings chronologically, instructing people to live one way during a certain period of their lives, and then differently during another period. And while these instructions were initially given in the ancient past and in India specifically, they still have relevance today.

Students, for example, are encouraged to live simply and frugally. They're supposed to be learning, not spending. The same is true for the elderly, who have worked all their lives. Old age is a time for casting aside material possessions (downsizing), living in a contemplative manner, and getting closer to God (maybe because you're getting closer to actually meeting Him, I don't know.)

But in the householder phase of life, where a person marries, has children and participates fully in the world, it's time to make money, to create and enjoy wealth. This doesn't mean that you cheat, steal, or participate in an unsavory or illegal occupation to gain wealth. Wealth is achieved through 'right action', a concept that can mean both 'correct' and 'honorable'.

Hinduism doesn't shrink from this economic reality. It embraces it. Hindus even have a Goddess of Wealth, and her name is Lakshmi. Many Hindu homes have a shrine dedicated to her. Daily rituals are conducted, and daily prayers whispered in earnest, requesting that she bless the household with prosperity. She is also welcomed into homes with family ceremonies conducted at the end of Diwali, an annual festival celebrated by Hindus in the fall of each year.

While these practices and traditions may seem materialistic and greedy to some, they are not. We live in a world where money plays an overly important role in our lives, most of the time because we feel we do not have enough of it, or worry about losing what money we have. Viewing life in this candid context, praying for wealth does not seem so selfish.

These three considerations of wealth in Hinduism may be the most beneficial to us: first, the acknowledgement that wealth is important in our daily lives; second, that we need to work to acquire it through legal and ethical endeavors; and third, that we must maintain our spiritual equilibrium and integrity once we acquire it. We should use wealth the change the world for the better and not allow wealth to change us for the worse.

To help us be open this perhaps new way of thinking, we would be wise to consider the source, as well. The history of India is a rich one, and its contributions are legion. The decimal system in mathematics, algebra, trigonometry, and calculus originated there. The science of navigation was an Indian innovation. India was also home to the world's first university, established in 700 BC, and gave us the game of chess and the world's earliest known school of medicine, Ayurveda. Its ancient Sanskrit is considered by many to be the mother of all European languages. A comprehensive list of India's influence and impact on the world's progress would warrant a book of its own, not just a paragraph in this one.

Suffice to say, in terms of science, mathematics, art, literature, and philosophy, India is a colossus of wisdom and knowledge. It was, and still is, an incredibly wealthy country, despite the images promoted by the mainstream media that would tell you otherwise. Political turmoil and foreign invasion have destroyed and displaced some of this wealth, but history has a way of ebbing and flowing. The Hindu culture's deeply imbedded philosophy of wealth is alive and well in its people, and as future events will surely bear out, it will once again flourish in all its glory.

The practical matter at hand, however, is to uncover, define, and articulate this philosophy so we can use it for our own improvement and enrichment. It was with that thought in mind that I recorded my conversations with a fascinating, intelligent, and passionate man. He shared his own personal views with me, steeped in what I learned to be ancient, mystical wisdom, for no other reason than to have me share it with the world.

The result, captured in random hotel-room conversations, late-night emails, and pre-dawn phone calls over a period of several months, is a rare jewel indeed, and I'm grateful to be a part of...

The Hindu Way to Wealth.
Byron Tully

# CHAPTER 1

# WHO ARE YOU?

*"It is when you do not know that you are free to investigate."*

*- Sri Nisargadatta Maharaj*

"**W**here should we start?"

"There are a lot of concepts that people have to understand, but it's like asking directions from somebody on the phone. 'This where I want to go.' What's the next question? The next question is, 'Where are you right now?' And that's different for everybody. Everybody's in a different place in life. When I try to help an employee do better, I first have to have a clear picture of where they are right now.

"What is their daily existence? And it doesn't exist in a bubble. They work for me. That's one part of it. What kind of work they're doing, how well and how fast they do it, and how they work with others, coworkers or customers. Their home life affects their work. So if there's a problem, or if you want to improve performance, you have to get into their world."

"Every reader of this book will be in a different place, geographically and personally."

"Yes, and we can't see that, so we ask questions. Every reader answers those questions to themselves, honestly, and they get the solution for themselves. So, I think the first question is, 'Who are you?' How people identify and label themselves is the first step inside their world. 'I'm a manager of so-and-so department.' 'I'm a son, husband, and father of three children.' 'I'm Indian.' 'I'm an Indians fan (Mumbai's cricket team).' That's the superficial part, easy stuff. Then you go deeper. 'I'm someone who's good at math, but I'm not creative.' 'I'm not pretty. I'm not smart.' 'I'm good with languages.'

"These are the characteristics that we've come into the world with, a little, but more of it is that we've had put into our heads from birth by parents, relatives, siblings. Any psychologist will tell you this stuff. But it all knots up and forms your identity. And most of it is an earthly perspective. It's not a spiritual perspective. Sure, God gave us certain talents: 'Here, you're going to be great with music. This is your gift.' No one can deny that. Genius cannot be denied. It just is. It's obvious and pure and overwhelming, beyond argument. So shut up, admit it, enjoy it, and use it. Just don't deny it because you look like a fool if you do. And if it's your genius and you're not using it, you're miserable and in poverty, financially and spiritually.

"So you get your gifts from God, but you get your limitations from humans. If you want to start to change yourself, the first thing is you've got to identify yourself. You make your list: this is me, the good, the bad, the middle. Not a wish list, a true list. Then you go to a close friend who's not toxic or negative, and ask them, 'How accurate is this?' Most of the time they'll say,

'Yeah, you're like that,' then they'll add, 'but you're really great at this, and your biggest problem is this.' And you get two or three friends to tell you about yourself. And maybe a parent, maybe a priest, maybe a professor who knows you and your work. And you get a 360 degree perspective of how you are seen in the world. If you get some really good information, some of it hurts. But that's where you start to work.

"That's your earthly identity, what you're identifying in yourself, what others see in you, and what you're presenting to the world. You're not asking for compliments or asking to get mugged by your friends (emotionally) when you do this. That's a baby step. You've got all these knots of string laid out in front of you. And you can do this with yourself, as a person, as a company, or a country, doesn't matter. Some people answering will have an agenda, but if three people tell you you're a jerk, it's not an agenda. You're a jerk (laughs.) Everybody wants to change. But nobody wants to accept. If you miss accepting how you are right now, you have a hard time changing.

"Personally, I want everything right now. I'm very impatient. When I realize this, I can become aware of it. Then I can change moment by moment in my life, if I accept first. It doesn't mean I accept that things will never change, even though some things about me and the world will never change, but I'm aware that this is the present condition. If you don't get your feet planted there, you can't take a step in any direction."

"That's pretty straightforward stuff."

"I'm not finished! That's only half of it, not even half of it. We have a greeting, Namaste. You've heard of it probably. 'I bow to the divine in you.' That's the other part of your identity that most people never acknowledge or maximize. You see God as being in heaven or outside of you, and you're trying to work to reach him, like Adam on the Sistine Chapel (laughs.)

"I see God as being inside of me and I have to work to let him out. I see myself as A Little Piece of God on Earth. That is my identity. So I take those characteristics. I can create anything. I can love everybody. I'm not God, that's just crazy to think that. So I don't judge anybody. That's somebody else's business that takes care of itself in this life or the next, much better than I could do.

"I work like God works, constantly, effortlessly—sometimes (laughs)—abundantly, not watching the clock, not measuring the results. 'Oh, okay let me see how the Himalayas are looking...how many peaks do we have now...?' God doesn't do that. He just creates. Boom! 'How do you like that volcano?'

"No, just create. Just love. Just give. Bigger, more, better, more highly evolved, more beautiful, but simple. And you let Him out through work and meditation. Or at least that's my way. Some people volunteer and do charity. Some people sing and chant. People go to temple or church once a week or once at the holidays and say, 'Oh, I'm worshipping today.' Great, I worship every day with every action. That's my offering. Who do you think has more of a chance of touching the divine like Adam?

"And if I can't see a certain action as being a kind of worship—even with cheering my football (soccer) team—then I don't do it. Or I try not to do it, because it's not worthy of me or God. It's that simple. God inside me, how's he going to get out? Look at that, get busy. Meditate in the morning and then go, whatever task you have right now. Go. That's the oil on this thing. When you oil it up, you can change it easier.

"It's greasy, like a car wheel. You had the problem with drugs, that gets slippery and falls away because you're a little piece of God, and even a single molecule of God doesn't need anything from the outside, nothing artificial. Does God care what other people think? No. He loves and creates.

"And then you let your choices be made freely, with the intention of making you happy, because happiness is your open communication line to the Divine One. This isn't selfish, and this isn't crazy. Some people say, 'Oh, when I'm rich, I'll be happy.' Okay, maybe you will. But you'll be much richer much faster if you get happy first. How do you do that? By being happy now. People think that being happy for no reason is phony. It's not phony. It's the natural state. You've just got in the habit of being unhappy. People think they'll be happy when everything's perfect. No. Be happy. Then things will move toward perfection.

"And this isn't to say you can go and do anything you want. If you're married, you can't say, 'Oh, I want to go sleep with another woman.' No. You have to think it through. You want to be happy, right? You think you're going to be happy upsetting your wife? No, you might feel good for a little while, but happiness is a bigger concept. If you think you'll be happier without your wife, then that's a long road you're going to get on. You better think it through. You might feel good quitting your job you don't like right now, but happiness is not in a single choice. It's in a procession of choices, made consistently and thoughtfully, that move you toward being a better person: moksha, liberation, the final goal. Within that is doing your duty, enjoying life, creating wealth."

"Being happy isn't making choices that are easy. It's making choices that are honest. Like emails that anyone can read and you won't be embarrassed. 'Yes, this is the choice I made. I can live with it with a clear conscience. Put it on the front page of a newspaper. I don't care.' You think it through, consider what's important to you and the people you care about, and make your choice. That creates happiness, and in that mental condition, you create things that are much more original, much more profitable, and much more long-lasting, than any other way. Happy first."

"So how does this fit into changing your identity?"

"Oh, I think I was going off the topic."

"That's okay."

"Okay. In the Bible, it says, 'God was the word, and the word was God,' and He said it, and it happened. Right? Something like that. That's the power of the word. You oil it up with meditation and worship, then you start to take things on your list and say, 'I'm this way now.' Affirmations, prayers, whatever you want to call them. And you just repeat them like mantras. People tell you things your whole life and you believe them, true or not, they become true for you. That's your world. That's your identity.

"So take that repetition and say something new about yourself. You say it. Say it again. Say it again. It becomes true for you. It becomes your new identity on this earth. That's the new you. You're a new product, if you think commercially, and this is your slogan. Only the point is not to sell it. The point is to become it. And what you're becoming is a better person. That's the best way to use things. To become a better person, and to make the world a better place. Because you do one, you're really doing both.

"People think they can say anything and it won't matter. That's wrong. You're now A Little Piece of God on Earth. You can say hurtful and destructive things, and people say most of those things to themselves, or you can say good things that build everybody up. The thought, the word, then it's in the world as a thing. That's the way it works. You look across the room at a party and see a beautiful girl. You instantly say, 'I'm going to marry her.' And you end up marrying her. There are millions of examples. Sometimes it's just saying it once, sometimes you repeat it over and over again, and it becomes real for you."

"Take three things you want to change. That's plenty. Some you can do things in your daily routine to change, like losing weight means exercising and like that. Things in your mind, the psychological, that's where the work is because we've been thinking these thoughts for years and they've carved grooves in our mind. If you want to change your thought patterns, it's like skipping valet parking and going off the road in the mud. It's bumpy and dirty and you don't know where you're going exactly, but it's an adventure, and it's one you have to take if you want to end up somewhere else."

"People try that a lot in America."

"They try it everywhere! And most of the time they fail. You see it and here about it all the time. People come to work at a new job, and the first month they show up early, stay late, and they're on top of everything. Then they get comfortable, and the old habits come back in.

"The thing that's missing when people try to improve is purpose. What's the purpose behind the change? If you can ask yourself that and get an honest, emotional answer, you're half way there. Why do you want to make a lot of money, I asked this one kid. He said, "The other boys in school made fun of me, and I'm going to show them." Perfect! I want to hire that kid! He's got a purpose that's emotional, simple, primitive, and immediate. It's not the highest of motivations. It's not lofty or elevated. He doesn't want world peace, but he knows what he wants and he knows why he wants it. That's it."

"What happens when he shows them he's been successful?"

"Oh, it'll be a disappointment, of course. They won't care or won't even remember that they were mean to him in school. But the habits and drive and rewards of being successful will already have been in his mind for an extended period of time, so he won't know any different. He'll still work hard because that emotion from childhood will always be there, unless he does a lot of meditating (laughs)."

"So you take an inventory of yourself..."

"Take an inventory, decide what you want to change, but most of all, remember that you're a little piece of God on earth. You're changing anyway. Every day you wake up and the things that happened to you yesterday have made you different, a little or a lot. If you can be aware of how you're changing and point yourself in the right direction, you're a step ahead of most people. And nothing can stop a relentless effort in a definitive direction. It is impossible to push it back, to contain it, to dissolve it. Just know your direction, take your time, be persistent and patient, there's nothing you can't become.

"Most importantly, you ask yourself, 'How can I let the God within me express Himself today?' Then don't be afraid when you just start giving and doing and accomplishing and receiving, because it can be overwhelming, the money and opportunities that will come in (laughs.) Watch out!"

## Things Mahesh Wants You to Remember

* Ask yourself why you want to be a better person. List the benefits you feel you'll enjoy. Only your purpose will hold you through the challenge of change.

* Take a hard but fair look at yourself. Know yourself, and then articulate the direction you want to go in. The road map from where you are now to where you want to be will then materialize. Define the steps it takes to get there, and begin.

* Know and remember your good qualities. Let them blossom in your actions. Inventory things you need to improve upon. Attack what you feel is your biggest fault first. Start small and work daily to improve. Ask for divine guidance as you go.

* See yourself as A Little Piece of God on Earth before you strap on other labels like employee, mother, father, son, daughter, husband or wife. You'll find

yourself better in all those roles if you accept your divine identity first.

❀ What is the mantra for what you want to accomplish or become? It should be short and definitive. It is the concept that you'll repeat to yourself over and over again and take action toward consistently. The size and quality of it will determine the size and quality of your life. It will also determine how much work you have to do, and how much faith you have to have.

❀ Now, work backward. There are steps to achieve it. There are other people who have achieved it already. Research their lives and the path they took. Look for common denominators. Model your behavior and work habits to theirs. If you have the right goal, you'll be inspired to action.

# CHAPTER 2

# THE FUNDAMENTALS

*"I am proud to belong to a religion which has taught the world both tolerance and universal acceptance. We believe not only in toleration, but we accept all religions as true."*

- *Swami Vivekananda*

"So regarding the fundamentals of Hinduism, as you understand them, how can you present those?"

"Okay, there are four. There's dharma, which is duty, kama, which is pleasure, artha, which is wealth, and moksha, which is liberation. The most important one is moksha, especially to me."

"Why's that?"

"Moksha is liberation from the coming back again in another lifetime after this one. You live a life so well, so worthy, you get rid of your bad ideas and you burn through your bad karma, and you don't have to come back to go through it all again to learn your lessons. I don't want to come back because I don't think my next life could be any better than this one! (laughs)

"But the others are important, too, and you have to do them. Dharma is duty, purpose, whatever name you want to give it. This is just saying, 'Hey, if you're born into a certain position, or have a certain talent to give the world, you've got to do it, regardless of how you feel about it. So just shut up and do it.'

"People put too much emphasis on their feelings and not enough on their duty. No, I don't feel like getting up and going to work every day, but I do it, because I have a talent for business, people depend on me, my family depends on me, so that's it.

"And I'll tell you this: you've never really enjoyed a vacation like a rich man enjoys a vacation. I'll tell you why: because every day and every minute he's working and focused. So when it comes time to sit on the beach or whatever, there's nothing that's left. He's done all he can do, so to hell with it. I'm sitting here with my fruity drink and my silly straw hat. Don't bother me. That's the way you want to be.

"So do your duty. Second is to enjoy life. When you say 'kama' and 'pleasure', people think kama sutra and sex. And that's part of it, but it's a small part. It's really more about enjoying life fully, whether it's love, music, art, or having friends for dinner. I'm richer than most people because I laugh more than most people. The universe is laughing and joyful and expansive and creative. You want to match up with that. This doesn't mean you go out and get drunk and sleep with everybody, but you do enjoy yourself.

"The third thing is artha, which is wealth. This is creating wealth for yourself and your family so you can care for them, live life, not be a burden on anybody."

"The first question people ask when I've discussed this with them is why a religion that encourages wealth has so many of its followers in poverty."

"Oh, in India? Well, India has a feudal history, not a democratic one like America. So that's different. And it's not that we haven't had wealth. The British stole a lot of it, and we're still trying to recover from that, and we will. But don't discount a concept because it's not one hundred percent manifested in the world. Only gravity would be acknowledged as true if that were the case!

"And don't think that a standard of living reflects 'wealth'. America is poor in a lot of ways, even with your standard of living. People are starving. They don't have healthcare. Children are homeless. That may be a thing to say, 'So what?' to in India, but you're America, the richest country on earth and you can't take care of these things? That's a poverty and failure of your government."

"Centuries ago, the kings in India established cha-trams that took care of the hungry, the sick, and the poor. They had more wealth than you could calculate. They had more wealth than you could comprehend. And they spread it around to all their people. When the British came in, they made the kings stop funding the chatrams, and the people suffered. They're still suffering today because the tradition of charity has been lost on a lot of wealthy Indians. I make no excuse for that. It needs to change."

"The people of India are resourceful. They do more with less that any country on earth. Anyone will tell you that. I'm not just talking. So with a little bit of progress, our improvement will be unbelievable.

"India needs to develop its infrastructure, devel-op its educational systems, healthcare, a more efficient public section. And the corruption is just unbelievable, which you don't realize until you spend some time in a country where you don't have to pay a bribe to get the lights turned on.

"And you have to realize this about our country: a hundred years from now, even with great progress, there will still be men and women living like they did eight hundred years ago, working the land, living in a shanty, without education or medical care. But if your car broke down and you came to them needing food and a place to stay for the night, they would give it to you without hesitation, even if they had nothing for themselves the next day. That's India. We'll be modern in some places. We'll be ancient in some places. But our heart is everywhere.

"So there's a lot of things that need to happen in India to manifest a higher standard of living, and they're happening, some of them. But regarding the pursuit of wealth, it's necessary and good to get after it and go after it and enjoy it when you get it.

"People say they don't want money, they don't need money, money's not for them. They're lying. You know who doesn't need money? The sadhus on the Ganges who live from day to day, not knowing where the next meal is coming from, where they're going to sleep, totally dependent on God's blessing through the charity of strangers half the time. If you're not one of them, shut up. You want money and you need money. So let's get on with it."

"You sound angry."

"Our culture and our religion...it's not for sissies. It's for getting things done, living full speed. So you do your duty, you enjoy yourself—turn up the music in your car! Play it loud! Sing along! And you work hard to create wealth, doing what you love and what you're good at, which, despite what people say, are usually the same thing. You just have to do some thinking and researching.

"And then you do everything you can to live a life so you can achieve liberation of your soul from this earthly cycle of birth and death. That's what the books and brahmins will teach you. You have these cycles of creating your own karma, and then having to live with it in this lifetime and maybe the next.

"But if you act—and karma means action—if you act correctly, fairly, justly, nobly, then you can release yourself from the cycle. If you don't, then you get to come back and do it again. And, I'll tell you this, that's the definition of hell: when you've been a jerk and didn't improve or repent in your previous life and now you come back. You don't want that.

"So the important thing you have to know is that life is about getting busy and getting after it. I don't mean everybody is a 'type A' run-around-all-the-time crazy person just to show you're trying to do your duty, create wealth, and get liberated or whatever. People have their personalities. You just can't be lazy. It's an insult to God who gave you this life. If you're quiet, get after it quietly. If you're gregarious, like me, be yourself, but don't just be loud. Accomplish something. You don't get to be a sofa potato."

"Couch potato."

"That either. I tell you this, and other people will tell you this: Indian people are the hardest working people on the planet. No argument. So if people are trying to understand our ways, it's simple: you do what you're supposed to do. You live an upstanding life. You enjoy your life. You create wealth. You try to live in the best way possible so you have no regrets, nothing illegal, nothing immoral. It's not easy, but it's simple.

"What role does meditation play in your life?"

"It's a daily practice. You can't really be sane and work at any kind of productive level in the world without making some time to meditate every day. I do it first thing in the morning because after I have a cup of coffee and look at my phone, who knows when, or how, or where the day's going to end. I just don't know. It's great if you can get it at the end of the day as well, but I rarely do.

"At the end of the day, I'm like every other husband: I'm talking with my wife until we fall asleep, whether we're in the same city or not. It's always the same. 'How was your day?' 'It was crazy.' 'What should we do about our children?' 'We can't kill them now. They're too old and people would notice' (laughs.) Same thing as most parents. I tell you this: meditation will solve a lot of problems, and what it doesn't solve it will make you realize it's not really a problem in the first place."

"I will tell you this also: the more time you spend on the internet, the more time you need to meditate. The internet and computers wind your mind up, make it tight. Meditation relaxes it. You're jumping and clicking and cutting and pasting and linking and emailing, go, go, go. Great. That's work. But at the end of the day, you've got to relax it. Get back in touch with God. Gain some perspective. I do yoga in the morning, like a lot of people, Indians or not. Then I meditate after I'm breathing better and not stiff. I should be better about getting exercise, but I'm bad. If it weren't for a little yoga, I'd be dead. My wife makes me get out and walk a lot when I'm home, so that's good."

"The two-plus-two-equals-four basic thing to understand is this: if you want to be happy, if you want to be successful, if you want peace of mind, then your thoughts, your words, and your actions have to all line up and be consistent. You can't think evil thoughts then try to do good. You'll fail. You can't say one thing and do another. People will know. You can't act without thinking. You'll do something stupid. We see it every day. You can do also sorts of rationalizing and clever tricks with yourself, but this is it. Be honest with yourself. That's most people's problem: they're trying to be or do something that's not in line with who they are and what, at a very spiritual level, they know to be true and right. Or they're thinking something that's harmful to themselves and, of course, eventually, to others.

"So what you have to do is you pay attention to what thoughts you're holding. Everybody has heard this since they were a child. 'As a man thinketh in his heart, so is he,' right? Then you pay attention to the words that come out of your mouth. People think that a word isn't important, but the sound Om was spoken, and the entire universe was created. 'God said let there be mountains, and there were mountains.' The words you say are powerful. Then, you watch what you do, how you spend your time. If you have big dreams, big thoughts, and talk a good game of cricket, but you don't take action, you'll fail, and probably go crazy.

"Psychologists will tell you that conflicting emotions will wear you out over time. You can't act in conflict with your thoughts for a very long time. A peaceful person cannot be sent to war without bad things resulting. A hateful person can't just let things go for very long. They have to fight, be angry. But if you think, speak, and act in alignment, with consistency, you're happy. Your conscience is clear. You're productive.

"You think to yourself, 'I'm wealthy.' You think this regardless of your present circumstances. You look for things to be grateful for, things that are beautiful and abundant. That's how wealthy you are: you can look around at things they don't appear to be good and find the good in them. Then you speak like a wealthy person speaks, always with possibility and optimism. You're generous with your blessings to others. That's how wealthy you are: you can be kind. Then you act like a wealthy person acts: you work hard to honor the gift of this life. You maximize your brain power and mental capabilities. You give more to your work than it gives to you, right now, so the blessings will flow later. And when they flow, you give like you're the richest man on earth. That's how wealthy you are. Do you feel that feeling I'm talking about?"

"Actually, I do."

"That's what you get hold of and carry around with you every day. Not in an arrogant way, but with a mindset—first the mindset, then the manifestation will follow—with a mindset of a person who is living in an abundant world, full of wealth. You contribute, you participate fully, you enjoy."

"So let's go back to meditation. Does that help with the thought process, in the alignment of thought, word, and deed?"

"Absolutely. You clear out your own small, silly thoughts and you can hear the big thoughts from God. The pure inspiration of what somebody called the 'silent wisdom.' It's hard to explain meditation and how you feel when you do it consistently and how it helps spiritually. It's beyond words. You just have to do it.

"But the medical research on people who do it is quite articulate. Your body is less stressed. Your blood pressure goes down. You're more creative. Better memory. Depression doesn't exist in people who meditate. Mood swings, gone. It evens you out at a more joyful level, I guess is the best way to say it. I've seen brain scans of people who meditate and people who don't. You want to meditate."

"What's your yoga practice like?"

"To me, it feels really good and I'm certain, in my mind, I look like an Olympic athlete doing it. But if somebody ever took a picture of it with their camera, it would probably be the most pathetic thing ever filmed. I'm sure I look awful doing it. I'm so stiff naturally.

"But yoga is so simple. It takes just a little training, a little practice, finding your own technique or way you want to do it. The challenge is just doing it every day, or at least consistently. You can take a class if that helps you, or if you want to meet somebody to date. But a little space, a mat, and get busy.

"People think it's just stretching. It's not. Yoga helps your breathing and your blood flow to the brain and everywhere else. It opens up your spine, where all the nerves run from your brain to your organs. So the nerves, blood, and energy are more open. I'm not a doctor, but the benefits of yoga are there just like the benefits of meditation: consistent, free from side-effects, and holistic in the sense that everything is nourished and nothing is damaged.

"What people don't realize is that you've got emotions caught up in your muscles and your organs. Yoga releases those. It gets your heart rate up, but in a relaxed way, so you're ready for meditation. It's much better to do yoga and meditate than it is to take pills for being depressed and have surgery for your bad back.

"You can't trust western medicine to keep you healthy. It's too symptom-and-disease oriented. It's too caught up in the corporate environment, which is profit-centered. Pharmaceutical companies, all the rest, you want to avoid that. I almost always have a reason to support a suggestion that I have, but with this, this is the one thing I say to do just because I say so. Actually two things: yoga and meditation. Just do them."

"What's your diet like?"

"I have the luxury of having really good food all the time. But when I'm in America, I'm mostly a vegetarian. The food's just no good there. I don't care if you're eating at the Four Seasons, who the hell knows where the chicken came from or what it's full of. I don't eat beef, although beef production is increasing in India. I think that's a mistake. You spend so much money raising a cow to adulthood and then you kill it? Stupid, but hopefully there won't be a market for it. Lots of water, especially if you're travelling as much as I do, but anybody knows that.

"You've got to nourish your blood. Vegetables do that. There's so much information about diet out there that it's really a waste of time to talk about it."

"I think it would be helpful, as obvious difficult to become wealthy if you're sick from eating bad food."

"Okay, there's the first solution right the you talked about that in The Old Money Book. The first medicine is the food you eat. We have Ayurveda, which will give you the right diet for your body. That's the first prescription the doctor gives you. So there. In America, you feed your children things I would throw to a stray dog in the street. Then you wonder why you're overweight and have heart disease. Don't wonder.

"The first medicine is the food that you eat, okay? The second medicine is exercise, like yoga. The third medicine is meditation. The fourth medicine is laughter, or joy. The fifth medicine is family. The sixth medicine is your purpose in life.

"People think Lakshmi (the Hindu goddess of wealth) is just about wealth. She's not. She's also provides clarity of purpose. You think it's crazy, but I know a lot of white people who've prayed to Lakshmi for clarity of purpose, and they get it very quickly. It comes to them naturally and helps them a lot. Can I say 'white people'?"

"Sure."

"Non-Indians. She's an equal opportunity clarity provider. That's the disclaimer we'll use, until I can run it by the legal department (laughs).

"What people never think about is how food affects your state of mind. You think you're not feeling well, but, no, you're not eating well. You have too much sugar, and you get depressed. You have too much caffeine, and you're running around crazy or not sleeping well, ɔ you're tired and you need more caffeine. You think you've got problems, but your body is just reacting to bad food, and your brain is trying to tell you something's wrong.

"The reason so many doctors recommend the vegetarian or the vegan diet is that plants have a natural intelligence and life force. You can play classical music to a plant and it grows better; everybody's read about that. So when you eat a plant that hasn't been sprayed with chemicals, you get that intelligence, that life force, and it goes directly into your blood stream. You're nourished, not just full from eating a lot. And the animal products that are sold are generally not processed very well and not clean. If you know the farmer and can see how he raises the animals, good for you. If not, be careful."

## Things Mahesh Wants You to Remember

- ❀ Whatever your religion is, practice it with love, devotion, charity and tolerance for everyone else in the world.

- ❀ A natural spirituality resides in a very deep and sacred part of our hearts. It is sometimes mysterious and beyond words. But the purpose of it is very practical: to live a fulfilling life as you live, work, and enjoy your time here.

- ❀ When your religious leaders promote judgment and condemnation for, and violence toward, those who do not share your beliefs, ignore them. We're all God's chosen people, and peace is God's chosen way.

❋ When you're in touch with the divine, your problems don't go away, they just remain in perspective.

❋ Meditate. Meditate. Meditate.

❋ Worship with your actions. Lead with your heart. Do your duty.

# CHAPTER 3

# INVESTMENTS

*"You have the right to work, but never to the fruit of work. You should never engage in action for the sake of reward, nor should you long for inaction. Perform work in this world, Arjuna, as a man established within himself - without selfish attachments, and alike in success and defeat."*

*- Bhagavad Gita*

"The thing you have to understand is that your mental condition when you're investing is as important as what you invest in. If you're investing and you're fearful, don't do it. You're going to lose money. If you're investing and you're certain you're on to a sure thing, don't do it. You're going to lose money. If you've done your homework and your research, or somebody has, and you're comfortable and confident that this is a good thing to invest in, then you've got a chance to make money."

"You've got to know that risk and reward are doing an eternal dance. If you have more risk, you should have more reward. If you're looking at something that could be really, really profitable, you certainly have some risk, otherwise, someone's lying to you or it's a crooked deal."

"There is a season for every investment. I remember a long time ago, interest rates for savings were twelve or thirteen percent for Americans. That's a good return for a guy working at his job. Just stick your money in the bank and get the interest. But it's not that way now. Then real estate was climbing, climbing, climbing. Values were going up. People had jobs and you could keep places rented all the time. Then the bubble hit and people are suffering, losing their homes.

"There are trends and bubbles, fluctuations all the time. Some are short, but most of what you can learn to understand is long term. You can see something that's going to be profitable or go up in value. So you get a position in it. You ride it, and then you get out when the climate changes.

"Stocks will be good for a few years; real estate will be good for a few years. Precious metals will be good for a few years, and by good, I mean they'll increase in value and give good, consistent returns to you with a minimum of downside corrections."

"I don't speculate. I invest. Speculation is just a short term wager that something will change in value. That doesn't do anybody any good except you, maybe. Maybe you make a profit on paper. You have created no jobs. You've done nothing creative or productive. You haven't learned anything. You're not a better person. What are you going to do? Pay your taxes and then go buy a fancy car? Drive around to nightclubs and brag about making so much money in so short of a time with so little effort? Grow up. You got lucky, or you had inside information. There's nothing to brag about. So don't speculate, but if you do, and it works out, you have to take a large part of your profit and give it to charity, because you didn't work for it. God gave it to you, so you have to give it to the world. It's like that with everything, but speculation, it's like that times ten."

"You have to remember that many times you're an outsider, an outside investor. What I mean is that you won't have what insiders have. You'll never have as much instinct, information, understanding, or access as people who invest or work in certain industries on a daily basis. You'll be outside, buying stocks or whatever, and they're inside, working at a firm full of professional investors or working at the actual company you're investing in. They know the industry comprehensively. Regardless of the season, they make money, but outsiders only make money when that investment is in season. And if outsiders don't take their profits before things change, they get killed.

"Real estate and gold are generally good investments because there is a limited supply of both, and people need both. I'm not talking in speculation; I'm talking long term investment. The other thing is that God created land and God created gold. Man created currency and stocks and all that. Which ones do you trust? I consider gold and real estate to be divine investments, but people look at me crazy when I say that. Still, it's the truth.

"People think that currency like dollars or rupees or yen is money. It's not. It's a paper promise made by a government that says, 'This has a certain value.' When people stop thinking that it has a certain value, it has less value or it has no value. And that can happen overnight. So I have gold as a reserve if everything goes badly. So I don't worry much.

"And trust me: things can go very badly very quickly. The reason things go badly is that people ignore history. You keep printing paper currency, sooner or later it has no value. But governments do this anyway, which is why every currency in the history of the world has eventually returned to a value of zero. They put themselves out of business. That's when huge transfers of wealth historically occur between countries, families, and individuals. You can't be an effective businessman without knowing your history. You can't work your butt off for years and then have it go up in a puff of smoke. You have to read some history. It may not repeat itself, but it certainly looks familiar sometimes. And there's always warning signs."

"Prices can't go up forever in any asset class. There's always an adjustment. And you can't keep pushing people down in society. Sooner or later, they have enough and you have a revolution. A benchmark you can watch for and measure is when food prices take forty percent of a monthly household income. Then people take to the streets. It happened in France a few hundred years ago. It happened in Egypt just a few years ago. Nature seeks and maintains balance in everything it does. Men seek advantage over each other in many things they do. That's what gets things out of balance."

"First, people in the financial industry sense that the match is over for a particular currency, and, more broadly, for a particular society the way it is currently structured. So they dump the currency, liquidate what they can, and sometimes leave the country. It won't be safe for a while. Then the panic spreads to the business owners, who are in less of a position to liquidate and run. And finally, the working people on the street have a very vague, bad feeling that things aren't right. Then they realize that they're money is not worth what it should be, what they've been told it always was. Then they stop acting rationally.

"At that point, currency isn't worth the paper it's printed on. Gold alone has value, as it always has. So that's the baseline. The divine investment that restores the balance."

"Real estate has value because it grows crops to feed people. You can also build houses on it and offer shelter to them. So those things don't change. But back to the currency...then, the authorities wait for the smoke to clear, literally sometimes, reset the monetary system so things can function again, so you have a sound currency that people and institutions have confidence in, and the cycle starts all over again. But the general population has probably lost a lot of wealth and suffered a lot.

"The hope is that when the balance is restored, we live in a better world. Sometimes we do. Sometimes we don't.

"The wisdom is to see the cycles that life and business go through, learn to read the signs, and then invest with the knowledge that your investment is going to flourish at the start of a cycle, stall in the middle, and devalue at the end. You want to get out sooner than later, even if you appear to leave money on the table. It's okay to be a year too early, but it's no good to be ten minutes too late."

"Gold has an enduring attraction for humans that give it value beyond financial markets. It doesn't fade, rust, dissolve, or disappear. Gold isn't going anywhere.

It's eternal, it's magical, and it's been that way since the Egyptians and it won't change. Experts will tell you that it has no value as an investment. They are either lying or they miss the point. Gold is money. It's the foundation of currency. It's a store of wealth. It's not political. It has no religion. It has no expiration date. Governments hate it because you can own it and there's no record of you owning it. It's virtually impossible to tax, and it's good everywhere in the world.

"Right now, the government of India is trying to get the gold in the temples. That's wrong, but they want it. Everybody wants it."

"Right now, there's a manipulation involving the price of gold. I'm not going to go into who's involved in it, but a lot of people are aware of it. It's no secret. Gold should be about ten or twenty times the price it is now in U.S. dollars. But here's what you have to remember: no manipulation in financial markets lasts forever. The chickens eventually come home to crow."

"To roost?"

"That, too. It's all going to reach a natural equilibrium at some point. And when it does, India will be one of the wealthiest countries in the world because everybody owns gold. I'm not talking about the government; I'm talking about farmers and shopkeepers and office managers. They all buy as much gold as they can as often as they can. That's going to be a lot of wealth and purchasing power when the wheels come off this manipulation out of London."

"There's the old story of the two men who fled their country during a revolution. One packed a suitcase full of currency. One packed a coat pocket with gold coins.

When they crossed the border, the man with the currency went to exchange it for local money. The bank teller told him, 'These notes have no value. You're government doesn't exist anymore.' The man with the gold went, sold his gold, and started his life over.

"Gold also has value as something that you adorn yourself with, which Indians all do. It is a reminder of your wealth and abundance. It's portable. You can leave the country with it, most of the time. You think these aren't concerns for you, but you don't know the future. You think Argentina can't happen anywhere? You're wrong."

"What is your attraction to real estate?"

"Real estate is also made by God. It's necessary for humans to live. They have to have a house, a place to do business, and a place to plant crops. So real estate is inevitable. The question with real estate is: how can you create value in it? Obviously, you can take vacant land, build a building, and rent it or sell it at a higher price. Or you can lease it to a farmer to grow crops.

"The real money in real estate is beyond that, though. It's creating something inspirational where it wasn't before. A building or a place that moves people while it serves its purpose as a business venture. Architects can do this, but most of the time it's the developer. He says, 'I've got a vision. We're going to build a place that the people can really enjoy themselves in.'

"That's when the value of real state soars. When it moves people emotionally. They also say, 'Location, location, location.' Okay, sure. But you've got to have it being its best use, the right structure in the right place.

The right design. Population and demographics, sure. But really it's the vision.

"You also need to get the most leverage. You can have a piece of real estate and collect money from one tenant or from fifty tenants. Which is going to give you more cash flow? Which is going to increase the value of the property? These are simple things, but people don't think about them when they buy a property. 'Oh, I'm just going to buy a house and my family will live in it.' Great. I'm going to buy a building and my family will live in it, and so will ten other families, and I'll be rich. You'll be paying the bank your whole life."

"A few years ago, when India's economy started to take off and people started really making money, these wealth management companies from New York and London opened offices in India. They were going to get clients who had just made ten or a hundred million and sell them investment products likes stocks and annuities and all this. Most of the Indians didn't buy it. They stick with the old ways of buying gold and real estate, not having to wake up in the morning and check the indexes to see how much you're worth. Most of those companies closed their offices and went home. Most of the people I know have about half of their assets in real estate."

"You want to work hard and turn over your money and someone hands you back a piece of paper that says you own this or we promise to pay that in ten years when this instrument matures? Or you want to buy a piece of land that you can stand on or a bar of gold that you can hold in your hand?"

"What about people investing in themselves?"

"Oh, yes, that. People say it all the time, but it's true: your biggest investment is in yourself. When you say that, people automatically think about education, and that's true. But you also have to continually improve, even after university. The guys I know who are the most fanatical about this are the Chinese. The Confucian philosophy: always get better, always improve yourself.

"I think it was Flaubert talking about Balzac when he said, 'He was so stupid when I first met him, such an idiot. But he just kept writing and he never stopped working.' And Balzac ends up being one of the greatest novelists of all time. You can start out in a ditch, but if you continually improve every week, you can be on top of the world by the time you're an old man like me (laughs).

"I've watched a lot of people who work for me start to imitate me in some of the way they did things, and at first, it made me feel very strange and I became upset about it. Then, my wife says, 'Take it as a compliment, but watch what you do because they'll do the bad things, too.' But then I saw the value of it, after a while, and I realized it's an effective tool for improving yourself. Like you want to be a successful writer..."

"I do."

"Then I suggest you starting working like Balzac! (laughs). That guy just locked himself in a room and drank coffee, writing for days on end!"

"You're talking about modeling someone's behavior."

"Yes. Model their behavior if they're where you want to be, but don't lose the advantages you have already. You have something or several things that you can do better than anyone else in the world. Don't lose or forget those when you start to inventory the skill set of someone you admire. Just add on."

"People don't look at the hours in a day as a resource. I do. I don't have to sweat over every minute now, but I do pay attention to how I'm spending my time. You've seen me if I feel like someone's wasting my time."

"You're pretty short with them."

"Of course I am! And I don't apologize for that. I can't get the time back. Here, have a thousand dollars, because I can make that back. No, you can't have an hour of my time. If you've got something to sell me or tell me, you've got ten minutes to explain it and get my interest. Okay, really five. If you haven't organized yourself to where you can get the point to me in that time, you don't have a good idea or you're not up to speed to do business with me."

"People start to get a successful business or career and they start to ride on their laurels. Ride on your laurels? Rest! Rest on your laurels. Don't correct me (laughs). You can't do that. You have reinvest in yourself, reinvest in your business and expand, or invest in another business to give you another source of income and more net worth.

"You take a small part of your money and you get the luxuries for you and your family. You give some money to people who need it. But most of it you put back into the work. You just take money out and take money out, you get lazy and too comfortable. You have to be relentless. And you have to be generous. This is an honor to your family, your ancestors, and God."

## Things Mahesh Wants You to Remember

- ❋ Gold and real estate are divine investments because they were made by God.

- ❋ Risk and reward go hand in hand. No exceptions.

- ❋ There is a season for every investment.

- ❋ If everyone is shouting about how good an investment is, it's finished. Don't rush in or get out if you can. If someone is whispering about an investment, consider it.

- ❋ Emotion is a bad investment advisor. Instinct is a good one. Research is the best.

- ❋ You have to keep money moving all the time. You have to keep it working for your benefit, in investments, or for the benefit of others, through charity.

- ❋ Currency is not money.

- ❋ The quantity and quality of your investment in your spirit, mind, body, and business will pay dividends in terms of the quality of your life.

- ❋ Time is a precious resource and should be used just as carefully, if not more so, than money.

- ❋ It's not worth anything until you sell it.

- ❋ Hesitation is deadly.

- ❋ Don't be afraid to take your profit and 'leave money on the table'. Tomorrow, the profit might not be there. Actually, the table might not even be there.

# CHAPTER 4

# WHAT TO AVOID

*"Awareness alone will overcome illusion."*

*- Kabir*

**"M**y kids get depressed sometimes about things, typical childhood, teenager things. And I would ask them, 'What are you worried about?' And they tell me this or that, sometimes about school, sometimes about boys, whatever is troubling them.

"When they would tell me, I would come up with a solution for the problem: study harder in your classes, work harder at this, do that better. And then I would give them work to do so they could improve. Now, if I catch them looking sad, I ask them 'What are you worried about?' 'Nothing! Everything's fine!' (laughs). And usually it is, because I have taught them to replace worry with work.

"If you get busy every time you get worried, you'll solve your worry, or at least forget about it. You'll be too tired to be worried. You'll be too rich to be worried (laughs)."

"You've got to avoid having conflicting emotions about what you're doing. If you're going to start a business, you've got to eliminate all your doubts and go straight ahead. If you're going to get married, get married, commit to it. Make it a success. No half way measures.

"If you have conflicting emotions, you'll sabotage your efforts. Your doubts will make you not do your best, not remember things, not be on the top of things. You research, plan, meditate, pray, and then give it all you've got. Every minute.

"Every action you take in life is an expression of your belief system. Do you believe you can succeed? Then why are your efforts not the best? Why don't you believe? Did somebody tell you something and you let them tell you what is going to happen in your life?"

"So this goes back to a person's identity."

"Yes. Who do you see yourself as? You have to invest in yourself, believe in yourself, bet on yourself, almost to the point of being a crazy person. No one can tell you that you can't succeed. You deny the existence of anything but success."

"If debt isn't business related, like a loan to start your company, don't do it. And then get out of that debt as quickly as possible. Banks can be very bad. They always want to lend you money when you don't need it. When you need it, they want to have everything as collateral. And you'll have to show them your accounts when you want money from them. They'll know everything about you, and then they may not give you the money just the same.

"Credit cards are convenient, but, you know, I don't have to talk to you about that. Taking on debt for purchasing clothes and things is not believing in the universe and not believing in yourself. It stops the flow of energy. It separates your attention. 'Oh, I have to make this payment on this' rather than 'I have to be a success in this.' And it makes you pay attention to an expense, which you don't want to do."

"But you've got to watch expenses in order to be financially healthy."

"No, not for me. I only want to focus on making money. I never think about how much something costs to buy. I never think about anything but making more money, accomplishing the next thing, and enjoying life. Somebody else looks after the expenses."

"Your wife?"

"Not now. When we first started, she did it. Now it's somebody in my office. I let them watch every dollar while I focus on the next twenty million.

"The sooner you get somebody else to watch your expenses, the better off you'll be. Give them instructions and just watch the monthly or quarterly reports. Just make sure you've got more money tomorrow than you had today, or else you have to sit down, analyze the numbers, and make changes. Then you immediately get back to making money."

"You want to avoid having too many habits. Make hard work a habit. Make your spiritual practice a habit. Make being thankful a habit. Everything else you need to be in the present moment and really here on earth, in your life. Most people have so many habits they're just sleepwalking. Then something makes them wake up and half their life has gone and they don't know what's happening. Then they get angry and cry about it. You can't react quickly and be successful if you're not fully awake.

"Television is awful for this. I read somewhere where the brain is more asleep watching television than when you're actually sleeping. That's no good. Television has too big an impact on your subconscious and your belief systems. The moving images in color and the music and the persuasion, it's all too much. People say they aren't affected by advertising. They are. We wouldn't spend money on it if it didn't work."

"And you're on the internet all day, looking for what? Celebrities to tell you what's important? The media on television has its own agenda and they're giving you instructions. They don't call it 'programming' for nothing. They present you with an idea of yourself doing something, using a product or behaving in a certain way, and they repeat it. The news does this, too. Repeated images are coupled with recurring themes, and that becomes your reality, if you let it. Black Americans commit violent crimes. All people in the Middle East are terrorists. People in India live in poverty.

"Labels and illusions, products and propaganda, that's what they sell. They don't want you to become wealthier or healthier. They want your attention. And wherever you focus your attention, that's where you're going: to buy their product or believe what they want you to believe. Television and the internet are great places to get information and make money. That is about it.

"The media tell you so much all the time about what's supposed to be important. Very little of it is. You have your business at hand and what you want to accomplish. That's what's important. If, at the end of a long week of being productive, you want to watch a television presenter on some silly show, that's fine. Enjoy the relaxation, but don't believe what you see, and don't believe what they tell you.

"Like right now, the U.S. stock market is flying high, but in reality, the U.S. economy is stinking very badly. That means that there's an illusion and you should avoid it. When charts and talk and this manufactured excitement contradict what you see and experience first-hand, run for the nearest exit (laughs)."

"'Thinking outside the box' is starting to mean thinking outside the television, or thinking outside the computer screen, or the mobile phone screen. People are so focused on these devices, that they're missing the world around them.

"They make the mistake of constantly looking for something new to entertain themselves with when they would be better off looking for something worthwhile to improve themselves with. The things I'm talking about for this book aren't new. They are worthwhile."

"All the young people have the ear phones now, the noise in your head all the time. The answer's not there. The answer is in the silence. If I get a moment to just sit and be quiet, I take it like it was oxygen."

"What do you personally avoid with a passion?"

"Gossip and greed. I can't stand either one. Gossip is toxic. I just walk away when it starts, and now, people know not to talk that way around me. Greed is fear. You think there's not going to be enough for you. That's the thinking of a poor man. I'm not a poor man, and I don't want to do business with poor men. I want to do business with wealthy men like myself who know there's plenty for everybody. Not that we don't negotiate tough, but you want to be in business with people who are bringing more to the table, not just looking for what they can take.

"I also like things to be clean. I don't like things that are cluttered or dirty. Lakshmi comes into clean homes, not filthy ones. So one of the first things you do is employ somebody to clean your house, as soon as you can. It makes you a better person to hire someone, give them employment, give them responsibility, and give them dignity in work.

"The energy will move better in a clean home or a clean office, too. You're working hard and taking risks. You don't want the energy of where you work or where you live to be dragged down. You want it moving through clean spaces."

"You've got so many illusions, so much propaganda and disinformation out there today. You really have to retreat from it and be aware of it. It's difficult to have clarity about things if you don't."

"What do you mean by illusions?"

"Things that feel good but aren't good for you. You don't want to be the smartest person you know. You're in big trouble when you realize this. It feels good to be the smartest person. You can tell people things, and they're impressed. It makes your ego feel good. It makes your life not so good. You're not going to learn anything, and you're not going to be challenged. It's the beginning of the end if you don't change it quickly."

"I was really scared when I realized I had hired several people who were smarter than me. They were a lot smarter than me. I thought they were going to take my company and kick me out in the street for a minute. Then I realized that they didn't want the company. They wanted a paycheck. So I went back to feeling like the smartest person in the room because I'd hired them (laughs)."

"People are always surprised when I don't talk much."

"That you don't what?"

"I know (laughs.) Except for this we're doing right now. I don't talk much in meetings because I don't learn anything when I'm talking. I learn when I listen, and I learn when I ask questions, but nothing when I'm talking. So I avoid talking when I'm trying to gather information and make a decision. I also can't hear myself think when I'm talking, and I definitely can't hear the Divine."

"If you want to be successful, avoid the routine and the security. You have to be very comfortable with fluid situations in life. You have to be flexible. You have to be responsive and be okay with not having a road map. You have a general direction most of the time, and if you see something that might work, you go for it. If it works, great, good for you. If it doesn't you have to find out quickly what's wrong and if it can be fixed. You quickly get an instinct for what will work and what won't, once you've lost money or failed a couple of times.

"People want great success and they want it in a step-by-step formula. It doesn't happen like that. It happens in a moment-by-moment dynamic which is not a formula, but a current. Get in it, and it will take you wherever you want to go. Yes, there's preparation, but when it starts to happen, it's a like a river and you ride in it.

"And when you're in it and it's happening, your stomach is in your throat and you want to celebrate, but there's too much work to be done. You also realize that it's the current that's taken you to where you are and can take you on, but you can't get a big head because it's not really you. You're doing the action, but you're in this powerful thing that's propelling the results. So you get a different perspective.

"People ask how I made so much money. I saw the direction I wanted to go in, did the work, but I let the flow take me to the results."

"The flow being the universe?"

"Sure, you can say that. I hear people say that. I'm the captain of the ship, but I'm not the sails. I'm not the currents in the water, and I'm not the wind. Still, I get there. Owning your own business is like have a ship. You can use it to take you there. You can swim, too, but you'll get there faster in a ship."

"You have to take the concept of 'failure' out of your life. You have to be impervious to what other people think. I know an Asian woman who invests in companies that she thinks are going to be successful. Her failure rate is ninety percent. Nine out of ten of the companies she invests in are clunkers. But she's one of the wealthiest women I know because when the ten percent pay off—boom! She's made her investment back a thousand times. So is she a failure? Nine out of ten times, maybe yes. But the one that counts, no."

"You're going to have to be very careful about your friends and avoid the negative ones as you go through life. This can hurt and be painful, but it's necessary. Some people just don't grow with you and you have to let them go or figure out a way to make it a friendship at an infrequent distance.

"The contradiction to this is that, if you're lucky, you'll go get rich and have friends who are just clerks in a city office somewhere, and you're still close because you went to school together. They knew you when you had the skin problems on your face, so you can fly them in your Gulfstream and they still call you 'pimple boy', or whatever your nickname was then. You can't fool them, and they don't want anything from you. But they won't mix with your new wealthy friends that you meet in Davos or wherever. So avoid trying to introduce them. It won't work. That's your two lives when you start from one place and end up another."

"Avoid trying to save people from themselves. It almost never works. People say Indians don't give money to charity, and it's true. A lot of us believe that you're getting your karma in this life, so there's nothing we can do about it. That sounds harsh, but that's a popular belief. I give people opportunities more than I give them charity, but I do give. I can't pull people off their path and onto mine, but I can moderate some of their suffering as they figure it out.

"But most of the people you'll try to save aren't starving in the streets. They're just not being everything they could be or just hurting themselves for their own emotional reasons. One day, maybe, they'll realize it and change. Probably not. People are who they are. Mind your own business."

"Loaning people money, especially relatives, is an impossible thing to discuss, but if you can avoid it, avoid it. You lose your money; you lose the relationship. It's been that way since the beginning of time and it's not going to change. If you can just give somebody the money and forget about it, do that. But that's hard, even for me.

"If someone does ask you for money, and you're caught unprepared, ask to discuss it later. Then, get your thoughts together. I've read somewhere that you can ask them a few questions and deflect a lot of requests. 'What do you need the money for?' 'Am I the first person you've come to?' 'What is your plan for paying me back?' 'What if that plan fails?' 'Do you plan on taking any vacations in the near future?' And then you say you'll think about it. A lot of times, if they're feeling entitled to the money, they'll get angry, say you're interrogating them, and just go away in a huff. Sometimes they'll ride it out. Either way, the real intention and the authentic emotions eventually come to the surface.

"If you want people to pay attention to what they're saying when they meet with you, take notes. It will help you remember and analyze, but it will also make them realize that what they're saying is going on the record. This will help you avoid a lot of hot air talk.

"It really just goes with the territory of being rich: trying to figure out when somebody tells you a situation is an emergency they need money for, and if it's not really an emergency, but an inconvenience or a problem they caused themselves. And it's almost always a problem they've caused themselves."

"The other thing you can do is just give it to them and bless them, hope that everything turns out alright for them. Give them love with the money and then forget about it. If you can do that with a clear conscience and an open heart, you're a much better person than I am because I can't do it. I'm sorry, but I'm honest with myself. I want people to improve. I'm not sure giving them money does that.

"I think my wife does it better and more often than anyone. I also think she does it more often than I know, which is fine. There's something really God-like about just giving instantly. I bow to that person who can lead with their heart spontaneously."

## Things Mahesh Wants You to Remember

* Trade worry for work.

* Mind your own business.

* Don't have too many habits. Be aware and awake as you go through life.

* Conflicting emotions sabotage your efforts. Get to the bottom of them.

* Take an inventory of your exposure to illusions.

* Ask yourself these questions: Is this really important? Is this propaganda or misinformation? Is this trying to tell me who I am and what I should want? Why am I being told this? If I accept this to be true, will it limit me?

- There's a flow in the universe that brings everything you want to you and you to everything you want. Jump in it with joy, passion, work, and abandon.

- Defy the entire concept of 'failure'.

- When you are afraid, consider the emotion an alarm. You may be facing an illusion. Deconstruct the fear. Boil it down to a choice between options that you can take action upon. Make your choice. Act without fear. Move forward.

- Don't loan money. If you can't afford to give it, refuse the request.

- If you can afford it and can give without resentment, do so.

# CHAPTER 5

# WHAT TO EMBRACE

*Everything comes to us that belongs to us if we create the capacity to receive it.*

*- Rabindranath Tagore*

**"**If you had five minutes to share your ideas about wealth with somebody, what you would you tell them?"

"The universe thinks bigger than you do, so let it. Don't put limits on what you can do. I'd almost say don't set goals, just articulate concepts, but you set goals when you start out so you can measure your progress.

"Don't do things for money. You'll only do so much that way, and when you get the money you thought you wanted and you thought would make you happy, you'll stop. Then you have nothing because your reason for doing what you were doing was finite and tangible. The universe is not finite and it is not tangible. So don't mess with the opposite of the universe. And it's very dangerous to accomplish a goal and not have another one waiting. You get yourself into big trouble when you've succeeded beyond your dreams. That's why I say, instead of having a goal, have a dream or a concept of what you want to be. Have your duty that you perform for God and mankind. You can keep becoming and contributing long after the money's been made and whatever goals you had have been accomplished."

"There was this study they did with children years ago, I think. They said, here, do this work. And the kids did it and had fun doing it and did it a long time and were really happy when they finished it. Then they said next, okay, do this task and when you get to this point, you get a reward. So the kids did it, but they did just enough to get the reward and no more, and they weren't as happy when they finished. Just do the work."

"It sounds like the concept of detachment in Hinduism."

"It is. You can't be attached to the fruits (of your action). You should enjoy them, but if you like them too much they become another illusion. I see all the secretaries with their designer handbags. They have the illusion that buying this handbag will give them the lifestyle, or show others that they have it. This luxury lifestyle of adventure, luxury, you know, what the magazines sell you. No! Not at all. You just have an expensive handbag and you're still trying to pay the rent. That's where illusions make you suffer: when you get attached to the fruits of your labor. And it can happen with a secretary or a millionaire: the 'boys with the most toys' and all that nonsense. You have to embrace purpose."

"The other thing to understand is that leisure time with family and friends is important because it allows you to disconnect, to detach, from your efforts and let them go out into the universe. When they go out, they blossom and come back to you in the form of wealth, success, or whatever."

"You have to embrace hard work if you're going to be successful. You can't look at it like something you dread. You have to commit yourself to it passionately. You also have to get, at some point, some idea of what the requirements are for what it is you want to accomplish. If you're going to be a doctor or lawyer, you need a degree and a license to practice. So you have to get good marks now. That means study. So that's what's required.

"How much do you have to study? You have to study hard enough to make the marks, and if you really want to excel you have to master your subjects. You have to know beyond the requirements. And the ultimate knowing is becoming. You've decided to be a doctor? You've studied at the feet of the best surgeons in the world? You know everything a doctor should know? You'll become a doctor. It is inevitable.

"In business, you don't have to have a degree, but it helps. You have an idea and instincts...you can make a certain degree of success for yourself. The path is not as clear cut. You can work for big companies, start your own, or be partners with somebody.

"I knew a man. He had no education and lived in the country. He went to the train station near his farm, and he waited on the train. The rain started, and most everybody got wet. He saw this, and went to the magistrate in the village. He said, 'I want to build a shelter for people when they wait for the train.' The magistrate said, 'We don't have the money for that.' He said, 'I'll pay for it. Just give me the permit and a lease.' 'Okay.'

"So he takes wood from his farm, builds the shelter for people with some benches and a little extra space. He goes to a local merchant and says, 'You sell tea. You want to rent space and sell tea at the train station?' 'I can't afford the rent to start that,' says the merchant. 'Don't worry. First month's rent is free so you can get started.'

"So now he's got a tenant paying money. Two months later, he has two tenants. Then they asked him to build a shelter in the next village. Five years later, he's a real estate millionaire. I know him. He's not a smart guy. He just saw what people needed and gave it to them. And he didn't let things get too complicated.

"That's one way to create wealth. The other way is to put yourself in the ultimate position."

"What's that?"

"That's when you locate an opportunity, which can be a company or a person or just an idea, and you provide resources or expertise to that thing in exchange for a piece of things in the future. I guess that's the best way to say it. You can invest in a company that's just in someone's bedroom. You get a position, at a very low price, maybe a sizeable percentage of the company, and then you help it grow.

"This is what venture capital or the stock market is: getting a piece of the action. The sooner you find a company, though, the better deal you get. The work here is a lot of work, too. Don't think it's not. You have to find the company, get a position, manage the growth, and then know when to get out, if you're going to get out. Technology start-ups are the most common type of this thing because the upside is so huge, but you can do just as well with the brick-and-mortar businesses. The real consideration is twofold: what is the product or service, and who's the guy behind it?"

"It sounds funny to talk about creating wealth. I'm saying you have to be strong and focused and determined and all that, and you do, but you have to embrace contradictions, too. That's the tricky part of having a philosophy: it can be turned on its head and still have value to somebody somewhere. Like you think that you have to be frugal to be rich, and I know the biggest spending guys in the world and they're some of the richest guys in the world. They have to throw money around, or they'll just die!

"So whatever you believe or whatever you're certain you know, there's a contradiction to it somewhere, that's alive and well and doing just fine. If you're dogmatic, it will make you crazy or violent. If you're accepting of contradictions, things you can't explain, then you'll do fine."

"You have to celebrate frequently. Get your family and friends together whenever you've accomplished something and have a good time."

"This book business is getting to me."

"Why do you say that?"

"Last night, I'm sleeping and I wake up suddenly. I'm thinking 'passion' and 'compassion.'"

"Meaning what?"

"I didn't know at first. Then I can't go back to sleep so I just get up and make some tea. Then I think about it. I think you have to have passion for what you're doing, the work you're doing. Then you have to be compassionate to the people you're working with. People think being a boss is ordering people around and being in charge. It's not. It's being the leader of a team.

"You can't do it all, and you need people. The hardest thing to understand is that not everybody is you. This isn't their life. This is their job. That's all. So compassion is necessary, just as the gods are patient with us. If I do it right during the week, my passion inspires my people to work harder. And if I really do it right, when they don't meet my expectations, my compassion inspires them to try again."

"I don't know if you want to print this or not, but I tell you this, just so you'll know I'm not just a numbers guy who's only in the material world. If you're working hard and doing everything you can do to make a success of things, there's going to come a time when you've done all you can do and it still looks like you're going to fail, or lose money, or whatever. Things are going badly. And then some coincidence or some luck or some 'thing' is going to turn around out of nowhere and change everything for you. That's the spirits or angels or ancestors or whatever you want to call them. They're real, and if you let them, they will come to your assistance."

"You've had this happen to you?"

"I have. A guy didn't want to do business with me. He had no reason to do business with me. We met. I gave him my best presentation about what we could do together, and he had a reason, a sound reason, for every position I put to him. He didn't need me. And he was right. I hadn't seen it from his point of view, which was a fault on my part. I only saw what could be in it for me. That was a hard lesson, but I learned it. And without this guy's business, at that time, I didn't know what I was going to do. I knew what was going to happen, which was, I have to close my company maybe, sell my house, go to work for someone else, a real disaster.

"So I knew it was over. He's on the other side of the table from me. We shake hands and he's about to leave. He walks toward the door, but he doesn't go out the door. He walks around the conference table a little funny in a way and then stands in front of me. I don't know what to think, so I just say, 'I thought you were leaving.' And he says, 'I thought I was, too, but I was just guided back over here.' So we laugh a little strangely, and I just hold my hands up in the air and say, 'I gave it my best attempt.' And he says, 'Forget about the presentation. Tell me about what you want to do.' So we sat for another hour. I told him what I wanted to do, not relating to the presentation, but another thing, and he likes that idea. So we were partners and made money together, all because something walked him back around to my side of the table.

"When you've given your best, I'll just say it this way, things outside your understanding will come to you aid. And I'll tell you another thing, when we shook hands and he left, and I knew we were going to be okay, I tell you the truth: I closed the conference room door and locked it, in there all by myself. Then I fell to my knees and thanked every god, ancestor, angel and spirit I could think of! I didn't want to leave anybody out! Whoever had helped me just then, or didn't help me, so what! I was so grateful! A little scared, you know, but so grateful."

"Getting a grip on some values, in the sense of what's important to you, is really important as you start to make money. There are so many temptations in the world that can destroy you if you don't know what you stand for. Every woman in the world will want you when you're rich. How are you going to behave? Every crook in the world will look for the opportunity to trip you up and blackmail you. People will come to you with ways to make money that aren't ethical, but may be they're legal. What are you going to do? If you wait to think about and come up with something in that moment, you are in trouble.

"You have to know now, decide now, commit now, and do right now. I like the values you talk about in your Old Money Book. They're the same all over the world. They're the same throughout history. Sometimes you hear them called Sacred Values. You give those to your children, you're okay. Give them money, don't give them money, so what? Don't give them values, you can be a billionaire today and your grandchildren will be worth nothing. And I mean that both ways."

"Here's how to solve any problem you have: meditate about it, work on it, and remember, people with less intelligence than you have probably done what you're trying to do. So have faith."

"I heard a guru on YouTube the other day. He said that wealth equals the life force you're sending out into the universe. I think that's a pretty good way to say it. You've got to embrace sending that life force out in the form of work, concentration, and gratitude, to make it really add up to wealth."

"You do have to embrace luxury. The universe is a magnificent place, huge, awesome. It's not scraping by and living hand-to-mouth. The earth is the same. The

Great Barrier Reef, the Grand Canyon, the rainforests, the rivers and oceans...there's abundance and affluence everywhere, so you have to mirror that in your own life."

"How do you do that if you're on a limited budget?"

"Stop thinking you're on a limited budget! Stop thinking of limits! Imitate the universe. Imitate God. You make me crazy with your limits! Every time you, Byron, think about limits, I order you to instead think about luxury.

"So the first luxury is security, having a safe place to live where you don't have to worry too much about violence. It's a crazy world, but we all want a safe place to live.

"The second luxury is cleanliness. Money doesn't want to visit a dirty home. Clean it, and as soon as you can afford it, have someone clean it. Create employment for another person. That's something rich people do. You'll become a better person, a better employee—because now you have an employee and you see all the things they do—and you'll be more sensitive to people's feelings. They're having a bad day, not doing their best work, you encourage them, but you have to be patient. And I'm better at talking about this than doing it (laughs). I've said this before maybe but I want it in the book twice.

"The third luxury is sharing with family and friends. You've got a billion dollars and nobody to laugh with, you're poor. You have to be generous to be rich.

"After that, the fourth luxury is to be free from worry, and you can do this anytime you choose. I know guys making a million a year who would trade it all to make forty thousand a year doing what they love, but they don't have the courage. Or their wife won't let them (laughs). They worry about their life because they're not happy."

"Did you make a list? Are you reading me 'Mahesh's Luxury List'?"

"I am! 'The luxuries of life'. I thought of it last night. I think it's very good. The fifth luxury is beauty. You want fabulous fabrics, candles with nice smells, and fresh flowers, all around you all the time. This makes you happy, keeps you happy, calms your mind and makes you feel good after working hard.

"The sixth luxury is doing what you love for a living. That's the best feeling in the world. You also want to have control of your time, have choices.

"The final luxury is having the best of everything. It's that simple. If you're going to buy something, make sure it's the best."

"I heard someone say that if you buy the best, you only cry once."

"Oh, that's funny! And so true! Can you write it so people will think I said it?"

"No."

"You're a very hard man (laughs)."

"So how is luxury different from extravagance?"

"Extravagance is more than you can afford. Luxury is the best you can afford. Extravagance is doing it for other people. Luxury is doing it for yourself, like buying really expensive sheets for you bed. Nobody else knows, but you spend a third of your life in bed, so why not make it luxurious?

"Extravagance is the fear of poverty. That's what psychologists will tell you. Luxury is the natural state of the universe. Extravagance is trying too hard. Luxury is effortless. Extravagance is calculated. Luxury is spontaneous.

"The ultimate luxury is peace of mind. You know yourself, you know what you're here to do, you do your best, you make money, you share it with those you love, and go to bed grateful and happy. All the philosophy in the world, and that's what it comes down to."

"You have to be generous or you really can't count yourself as rich. You're just a guy with a lot of money who's worried about it all the time. I ran into a friend of mine at Ascot and he saw me and panicked. He had forgotten my birthday. So he just walks up to me at the party with all these people around, and takes his watch off, puts it on my wrist and says, 'Happy Birthday, Mahesh,' and he hugs me like he's going to squeeze the life out of me.

"I thank him, and then my wife is looking at me like she's going to kill me. I say, 'What's wrong? He just gave me a watch for my birthday.' And she tells me that the watch was an anniversary gift from his wife and I've got to give it back. It's a nice watch, and I don't want to, but I know my wife is right. So I find my friend's wife by herself and I walk over and try to give the watch back. I say, 'He gave this to me for my birthday, but I think he's had too much to drink and didn't realize that you gave it to him.' And she just smiles and says, 'Oh, you know he's always had too much to drink at these things, but he loves you, and so do I. I gave it to him with my heart, and he gave it to you with his. So keep it with both our blessings.' I start to get emotional just remembering it. That's generosity. That's love. My wife argued with his wife later, but it didn't do any good. I got to keep the watch. It's the only one I wear now."

"And here's something that Westerners don't like to accept, but you have to acknowledge it: sometimes wealth is matter of destiny, the karma from your previous life. A lot of people are going to work hard and be ambitious, but only a certain number will be rich. You can call it luck or whatever, but it happens.

"If you have some bad karma from your previous incarnation that holds you back, you have to work very hard and be very devout to get rid of it in one lifetime. And then we've got Padmini Vidya, which something you'll not understand, that involves past lives and ancestors praying and chanting for wealth to bless their children and grandchildren, even before they're born. You've got to get your punya up if you want to be rich! (laughs) And by wealth we're not talking about just stacking up money so you can say you have this much or that much. We're talking about directing the flow of energy that blesses people."

"Can you tell me more about that?"

"No. I'm not qualified, and the stuff is too powerful to discuss it without authority and complete understanding. But here's the other part of destiny: it's a contradiction, too. Destiny is sometimes what is going to happen, no matter what. It's also infinite intelligence knowing the choices you're going to make and seeing the end result. It says, 'Here, this is your destiny.' And it's not set in stone, it's written by your choices. And because infinite intelligence can see the past and future infinitely, it can see what choices you're going to make, and what your destiny is."

"Did your parents or grandparents chant and pray for you to be rich?"

"Somebody did. You know I talked about contradictions?"

"Yes."

"Here are some contradictions for you. I can look at economic data and tell you what's going to happen in a country or an industry in the next two years or five years, and I'm rarely wrong. I can look at the spreadsheet for a company and walk around its facilities for half an hour and tell you what the problem is and how to maximize productivity and profit, and I'm always right. I can talk to a person for fifteen minutes and know more about them than their parents or wife.

"Those are talents I have, but that's not what makes me wealthy. I'm wealthy because I think first about how we're going to make people happier or more productive by providing them a product or a service. What's in it for them, not what's in it for me. When I have a partner, I think of what he really needs from me—money or management or whatever—that's going to make him rich first. I do that, then, I'll be fine. When the money comes in from the businesses, I think of the employees or vendors who made a contribution. How can I honor their efforts with an even hand? Is it a compliment or recognition or a bonus or a salary increase? What's fair? Then I'll be fine. Do we need to reinvest? Can we expand? If we need to, we do that first. Then I'll be fine. When the money comes in from all that, I give money to my wife and set aside money to invest for my children, and, hopefully, one day soon, my grandchildren. Then I have charitable commitments I make. Then I have my-self. That's why I'm rich: because I put myself last."

## Things Mahesh Wants You to Remember

- Do what you love to do. Think big. The money will come.

- Know what's required.

- Be detached from the fruits of your work.

- If you can, put yourself in the ultimate position.

- Begin to define, recognize, and enjoy luxury today. Surround yourself with it. Your mind absorbs sensory images and reproduces the most frequent ones. Expose it to luxury.

- Avoid extravagance.

- Define your values and embrace them now, before you get rich.

- Destiny plays her part. Accept it.

- Put yourself last. The universe will reward you.

# CHAPTER 6

# THE WORLD WE LIVE IN

*"Yesterday I was clever, so I wanted to change the world. Today, I am wise, so I am changing myself."*

- *Rumi*

**"A**re you worried about the current state of society?"

"I keep it in perspective and try to stay informed, but remember: your mind is a sponge and whatever you show it gets soaked up. So I keep the disasters and tragedies to a minimum. I'm not callous, but what can I do? If my wife says this is a problem and we can do something effective, then we talk about it and something gets done, usually without any publicity. Otherwise, I'm focused on the good things in life, work, happiness, and the things I can do something about, like this email that just came in."

"People focus on all the problems in the world and protest and complain about them, okay, I understand, there's injustice. The 'one percent' people are all evil for being rich. No, your government has been purchased by major corporations and it's doing the work they've been bribed to do, which is making laws good for big companies. Class warfare is just a sideshow to keep you distracted.

"My companies are big, but they aren't Exxon. You want to tax the rich, okay then, do it. The rich will take their money and leave. You can't leave. You don't have the resources to live anywhere. The thing people don't realize is that they vote with their wallet. Apple has billions offshore that it doesn't pay taxes on, but you still want your smart phones. Fine. But I admire the people protesting in America. Their executives are horrible crooks, and I'm speaking as someone who has to do business in India! (laughs.)

"If you see a problem, take a positive action to correct it. Or take an action to ignore it. Boycott it. Find an alternative. Finding that solution could make you rich and a lot of people much happier. But you can't just look at the downside of everything. It weakens you. There's a solution to every problem, and if you start to work on it sincerely, whether it's a business problem or a social problem or a political problem, people will come out of nowhere to give you support.

"America's the best example. There's a natural disaster anywhere in the world, some people go on television and talk about it. Americans throw millions of dollars at it within hours. Japan, Haiti, Africa, wherever. I love it! It's so amazing! It's just them saying, 'We're so lucky. We live here in peace and prosperity. We've been blessed, so, here, take this money and rescue people, feed people, help people. We've got plenty and you need it.' That's so divine and universal."

"You talk about the 'one percent'. How do you feel about wealth inequality?"

"There's always been income inequality. So that's a reality. You have two people, and one will be richer than the other. That's human nature. It's a problem today because of the way the wealthy are behaving. Executives who are not owners are taking huge salaries, a thousand times their employees' hourly wage, and the companies aren't performing. That's not fair. It's not inequality. It's injustice. If a guy on the assembly line doesn't perform, he gets fired. So it should be the same for executives. The boards (of directors) are no help, either.

"Of course, I make a lot of money because my companies and my investments make a lot of money. That's the only reason. My income is big, but it's because the companies do well. The way they're structured, I'm going to take a loss if my companies don't do well. Also, it's the way some of these people are behaving. They're showing their wealth in a distasteful way while people are losing their jobs. They're insensitive. And that creates resentment. My life is very different from most people, but I try not to be out of touch. It's like between the way (rich) people act in Delhi as opposed to the way they act in Mumbai."

"The thing that the working people need to realize is that a lot of this is just a big story for the media. It makes headlines. Keep it in perspective: businessmen who are investors and entrepreneurs pay employees and provide goods and services. So we're not holding a gun to anybody's head. We have money, and we have responsibility. Hand in hand."

"A lot of my peers like to push costs down and wages down and cut jobs in order to maximize profits. That's short-sighted, at least for me, because, selfishly, I need people to make decent wages so, at the end of the week when they get paid, they can take some of what they've earned and go buy the things we make and sell. If they don't have any discretionary income, I'm in trouble. As a matter of fact, we all are. Needs are a small part of the economy. Wants are a bigger part. I pay people a little more than my competitors. I get to keep better people longer, but I also demand a little more from them.

"If I had my way, we'd have a huge middle class all around the world. That's where all the great innovators come from. High school kids with enough family money to sit on their rears in the summer and tinker with something in the garage. College kids who can pool their resources and start a company with their roommate. The 'rags to riches' story isn't as common as the 'suburbs to riches' story."

"What do you think people need in order to be upwardly mobile?"

"Capital and education. It's that simple. We do the micro-finance programs in India. They're successful. Don't fool yourself. You need money to start a business. You need money to get an education. You need money to invest in a start-up. Wages aren't going to do it. Wages are flat and have been for a long time. You aren't going to get out of this problem with wages. You're going to get out of it by seeking the divine, imitating the divine in its unlimited nature, and letting it blossom in your life. If you have your values in place, again, as you get more affluent, they you'll hold onto your money and your quality of life. But you've got to have both.

"You've got to be hungry for improvement. I'll tell you this: don't get in the way of an Indian woman who's just got a loan to start her small business. She will run over you, and anyone else, to be successful, pay that loan back, and be on her way.

"You also need education to preserve the wealth you create, like you talk about in The Old Money Book, or else you make the money and it goes out the window as fast as it came. People cheat you in investments or ask for money when you can't see their real agendas. You go to class and read some literature from two hundred years ago and see that people don't really change. You make money and someone comes asking for a loan very elegantly, and you say, 'Oh, he's like a character in that novel I read!' (laughs) All of your experience and learning come to the front when you start to earn money and see people come through the door."

"The best problems you have to solve are the ones in your living room, in your bank account, in your neighborhood. That's where the opportunities are. Don't send a billionaire a message on Twitter thinking he's going to help you. And the best opportunities are online because that's the most highly leveraged market on earth.

"You can have a neighborhood market and sell to five thousand people in the area, or you can sell things online and have a billion customers. You have to look for highly leveraged situations if you can find them. You may start where you are and start small, but keep looking. That's why Bollywood, Hollywood, Wall Street, London, and markets like that are so competitive. You have a single location and the possibility of a lot of customers.

"I don't worry that things look bad. Things have always looked bad, and sometimes they've been bad. You just hear about it instantly and all the time now with the internet. Most of it is just noise. Focus on wealth, work, family. You'll be fine. I know, easy for me to say, but I said it to myself over and over again when I was just starting out, and it happened.

"There is corruption in business and government. There's no way around it. I'm not going to preach about it and how you should handle it. We try to deal with it as it happens, with the reality of the situation. This is the water we're swimming in, as somebody said recently. Try to keep your head above water, I guess, and know that you're responsible for your own actions, regardless. I'll have to face my employees and my family if I do something. I keep that in mind and it makes difficult decisions a little less difficult, but they're still difficult."

"There's a lot of evil in the world, and I don't mean just misguided or misunderstood people. I mean evil, when you get to where I am and see all these people who are supposed to be at the top. In one sense, they may be, but they're below the bottom in so many other ways it's just frightening. My wife can't handle it a lot, so I do a lot of socializing alone. One thing I do try to do is be aware of it as soon as possible, get away from it as soon as possible, and go find something joyful to experience immediately."

"Love is the most powerful force on earth. Freedom follows it, like a little dog follows a boy. No matter what people plan and try to do to control the whole world, it won't work for very long because people love each other and want to be free. The 'Illuminati', whoever they are, will be defeated by the 'Goofanatti', a bunch of kids on skateboards who've painted their hair purple and get everybody to sing along to some silly song. That's the way the world is. You can spell 'Goofanatti' any way you want because I just made it up (laughs.)"

"The environment is in big trouble. I just got out of a company because we couldn't agree on how to change without the impact on the natural resources. But I'm not going crazy about it, maybe I should be. The earth is its own being. It's going to be tolerant of humans a little, then it's going to have enough and it's going to discipline us like children. It's going to protect itself. With global warming, you'll have a rise in sea level to cool it off. You'll have storms out of season to cool it off. You'll have disasters and droughts and floods to make us pay the price for our lack of responsible actions.

"People will have enough, too, soon enough. Bad food, sick children, polluted air. You won't be able to tell them, 'Oh we have to do this so everyone will have a job.' Their priorities are changing. They're evolving. You can't tell them the sky is falling anymore. It's not. You're greedy. You're falling.

"Wealth is going to turn a corner and become more spiritual in the coming years, after the Kali Yuga. What's best for everybody that still makes money? That will be the new formula. It won't be overnight, and it won't be an even transition, but that's the way it's going. There will still be exploitation and cheating, but it will change. Part of it will be necessity. Part of it will be a change in people's thinking from just awareness. If you become aware of something, you will have to acknowledge it. If you ignore it, you will become less of a person and suffer. If you acknowledge it, you can accept it or you can decide to change it in some way. If you decide to change it, as a person or a group, you will change it, probably permanently, and probably for the better. And you'll be a better person for participating in the change.

"Political revolutions happen when change that could help people has been too long in coming. It wasn't able to be done peacefully, and it was necessary, so now it has to be done violently. Or it comes when a few people in power decide that they can take control very quickly. You always have to be on the side of peace and freedom, even if it costs you you're money. If you're not, either because you chose not to be or you were negligent, then, no matter what you profit or preserve, you will not be wealthy.

"That's rare, though. Most of the time, it's the evolution of people and things: slowly better, slowly more fair to everybody, slowly more peaceful, slowly more loving, slowly less hating. With a few steps backwards and to the sides with wars and disasters, but the evolution is upward, outward, and better overall."

"Being a politician, people expect you to say a lot and do only some of what you say. That's the game, like dating a girl: promises, promises. Then you get married, and the truth comes out (laughs). Being a businessman, if I say something, I better deliver, to my suppliers, to my employees, to my partners, or I have to answer with a decrease of profits. So businessmen are in a position to create a lot of wealth and a lot of goodwill.

"If they do what they say, then they can speak from authority about problems that face the world that don't have anything to do with business. They can also direct profits to solve problems. Income inequality would be a lot less of an issue if the one percent followed Bill Gates' example with the foundation. But they don't. They're greedy. That's not wealth. Wealth is money plus everybody loving you."

"There is discrimination, and that's not right. When I'm in America, and I go to a store, the salespeople are slow to wait on me sometimes. I used to get angry, now I just laugh about it. They're living paycheck to paycheck because they judge people. I'm living blessing to blessing, one gigantic blessing after another, because I love people. Maybe that sounds like a snob, but I don't judge people by the color of their skin.

"In India, our women have been not treated well, but that's changing. I grew up in a very traditional household. The man was in charge. The woman obeyed. That carried into the workplace. But last year, as an example, a woman came in to interview for a job. She meets with two of my people, and they're just so excited about her. I look at her C.V. and it's good. Then I meet her and she's dynamic. She's smart. She's engaging. And I have to hire her because if I don't, one of my competitors will, and I'll lose out. Honestly, it doesn't matter what I personally think.

"That's one of the good things about capitalism: it knocks barriers down because people want to make money. You have to have talent to make money, and if the most talented person is a woman, that's it. You hire her. It was funny. She tried to charm me like she'd done the others, saying, 'You remind me of my father.' I just smiled and said, 'Tell your father you need to be in the office at 7:30 tomorrow morning. You've got a lot to learn about our products.' She's doing great for us.

"The second way capitalism is good is that it keeps the peace a lot of times. There would be many more wars if we didn't have trading partners. We have deals with countries, people we don't like, but we do business with them. So there's no violence a lot of times. Everybody wants to get paid, pay their workers, and keep going.

"But we also start wars to get access to other people's oil."

"And that's the most shameful behavior any person can do: kill for money. When I see the people and even meet them, and I know they're responsible for that, I just laugh and turn my face to the sky in gratitude. I imagine what karma has waiting for them, and I'm so grateful it's not me. One guy even asked me, 'What are you smiling about?' I just said, 'Oh, nothing.' He was a total bastard. But it's not my problem. You want to start a war, fine. The first people you send into battle are your children or your grandchildren. If you believe in your cause, you have no problem with that. If you don't, you need to take it back a few steps."

"Making money is good for everybody when you're not taking advantage of people and destroying the planet. So you've got to get all these thoughts about businessmen being evil out of your head if you want to be rich. Businessmen are focused. We want results. That's not evil. That's what it takes to be successful."

## Things Mahesh Wants You to Remember

◈ Focus upon and solve the problems within your sphere of influence.

◈ Don't hate rich people. Don't hate anybody.

- Everything is evolving. Be a part of that. Allow yourself to evolve into a better person and quietly accept that you've improved or see things differently. This will open doors of opportunity for more of all good things.

- Make sure your business is making a profit and making a contribution. Profit alone is not enough.

- You walk through the world every day. You may not feel you can change the world, but you can, to a certain extent, choose the world in which you will participate.

- Awareness is the first step to change, whether it's you, your company, or the world.

- Don't do bad things for profit.

- Be one of the good guys.

CHAPTER 7

# THE NATURE OF THE UNIVERSE

*Our truths discovered are but dust and trace*
*Of the eternal Energy in her race.*
- Sri Aurobindo

"I'm not quite clear on how the universe and the way it behaves relates to creating wealth in someone's personal life."

"The universe makes the rules, the universal laws that everything functions by. Let's start with the planets. Our galaxy, the whole universe: it was created and now it functions perfectly. Stars are created, planets are in orbit. Everything is in motion, creation, destruction, preservation, nourishment, it's all there. Everything is provided; everything is taken care of.

"So you have to get your mind to see that it's all in God's hands. I'm not talking this Christian God or that Hindu God, or Buddha or Allah. I'm talking the Supreme Intelligence that we're not going to put a name to, the impersonal, all-seeing, all-knowing, all-loving force that's in everything and around everything and beyond the outer edges of everything, eternal and invisible, that God. People can't get their minds around this concept, but you have to have some understanding about it, about its capacity, to establish a foundation of what you have to understand to be rich. The spiritual before the material, Byron.

"And that first thing is, God's got it covered, to speak casually. It's all taken care of. If He's created it, sustained it for a few billion years, and He's got the planets, and the galaxies, and all that organized, under control, then let's have a little faith. That's what I'm saying.

"Then, we've got earth. It's also in motion, just like the other planets, around the sun, but also rotating on its axis, and we have the change in seasons, also more motion; the tides going in and out from the moon, also in motion; the days going from dawn to night, also in motion; birds migrate, fish swim upstream to do their thing and then die; so it's all in order—unless we pollute it too much—and it's all perfect.

"Then finally, we have our bodies. We're born, we live, and we die. We're in motion. We're awake, we're tired, then we're sleeping. So we're in motion. We're eating, digesting, then we expel waste, always in motion. Our breathing is going in and out. Our blood is flowing, always in motion. You have a blood clot, and you could die.

"So this circular motion of the entire universe is a law. It's a cycle. It doesn't stop. If it does, we're in trouble, regardless of what aspect you're talking about: planets, earth, seasons, our bodies. When we work, we earn money, we spend money, we give money, and then money comes back to us again. It's a cycle. By holding onto money, you block the flow."

"So are you saying people shouldn't save money?"

"No. What I'm saying is that just in the same way you have a little extra food in the house or go to sleep before you completely collapse, you should have some surplus in your finances. But you can't just focus on stacking money up in a corner. It has to flow. It has to come and go. Who has more energy: someone who goes to sleep, sleeps ten hours, then wakes up and says, 'Oh, I'm going to conserve my energy and not do anything all day,' or the person who gets up after sleeping and gets busy, expending energy, keeping things in motion, working hard...?

"The person who tries to save and preserve will never have enough compared to the person who gets out there and creates and contributes. Wealth is the reflection of what kind of energy and how much of it you're putting out into the universe. There are also other factors: do you do what you do with love? Do you do it with detachment? Are you really doing what you're supposed to be doing? Do you think you deserve to receive as freely as you give?

"But seeing the Supreme Being from a universal perspective is key. If He's got the galaxies and the planets, He's got you covered, too. You're safe. Everything's taken care of. This is the basis of the faith that you have to have to create wealth. You've got to step out there when you don't see the next step, and know that you're provided for.

"And, in the absence of all visible evidence, you've got to continue to work and have faith because what you've got right now in life is the visible. What you're creating with your thoughts, words, and actions is, right now, not visible. But it will be tomorrow and in the future. You are in the constant process of becoming. There is no set condition. Nothing is static. Everything is in motion. And nothing is left without what it needs at every moment.

"So that's the universe and the way it works. This is physics. It's philosophy. It's nature. It's everything. Security plays very little part in the function of the universe. Faith plays the biggest part. People think they have security in money; that's an illusion. The only security is being in constant contact with the universe and understanding its operating procedures. I guess that's the best way to say it.

"You learn and go along with these rules, and life is easy. You stay ignorant or thumb your nose at these rules, and life will be hard. Life will break you because life is nothing but the physical demonstration of these rules and the choices we make with awareness of them, or in ignorance of them."

"Obviously, when you look at the universe and the way nature works in perfection, you see that the universe is intelligent. That's what you can't deny. And it's beyond a book-smart intelligence. It's an awesome intelligence. How can bumble bees fly when they're not supposed to be able to fly? How do a million things happen in concert with one another? It's all intelligence that is beyond human understanding, comprehension, or ability.

"We can't think this stuff up. When we try to play God, we fail. 'Oh, I never thought about that', that's what happens when we try to manipulate: something we didn't predict happens as a result of our actions. But the universe, because its intelligence has no boundaries, it sees everything and knows exactly what to do without thinking. Not without thinking, I should say, without hesitation.

"The other part of the intelligence is that it's not just intelligent about what it has created already. It's intelligent and aware about what you want to create. It's responsive. It listens to your requests, your hopes and wishes, and says, 'Okay, here you go.' Then you get what you asked for, maybe in the way you thought you would or in a way you never dreamed it would happen, and you're surprised. You shouldn't be! (laughs) You should be grateful, even if you realize now that you didn't really want it. At least you know that the universe is listening and you can create something now, with more wisdom, and go on and live better!

"People are constantly creating their lives and their level of wealth without realizing it. They're thinking about being poor and being afraid of that. They're talking about how bad things are. They're not working because they're not getting paid enough to work hard. That's their story, that's what they're telling, and that's what they're getting. It's no surprise, but you can't tell them any different. They think God hates them or is punishing them. No, the little piece of God inside you is doing it to you. You're doing it to yourself."

"This is the part of the law that's not a big blanket rule. It's personal. It shapes into your individual world. It is a universal law, but it is personal and unique to you. How you use it is different from how anyone else uses it or understands it. God is universal intelligence. He, or She, I should say, is also personal.

"You can go in your room late at night and whisper with your heart in pain, and God is there. You can go on the ocean and watch waves come at you that are tall as buildings, and God is there. You can go to a temple with a thousand people lighting candles. God is there, too. But it's easy to forget. He's the one boss you can still have as a friend! (laughs) You can't escape the fact that He's your boss, but you can ask Him to be your friend."

"The universe is intelligent, it's personal, it's constantly moving, and it's emotional, which is the strange part. You think with all the laws of gravity and momentum and all the science we see that it would be logical and precise. It is precise, but it responds to emotion. Love is the most powerful force guiding the universe. This is not some feel-good website blogger telling you this. This is me, the person who puts it into action on a daily basis with results you cannot argue with.

"I'm in the room with guys who make billions. We talk and dream and scheme up things. Sometimes we do them. Sometimes we don't, but I tell you this: the room is full of love. Everybody loves what they're doing. We love what we're talking about. We get excited and we make things happen, all because love is the driving force. There's no baby-whining in the room. There are questions and concerns, but there's no pessimism. The only thing I think my kids say that really makes sense is when I mention something, and they say, 'It's all good.' Yes, it really is."

"Being thankful is a magnet for your desires. Gratitude about the fact that you're living and breathing right now is the first step to being rich or whatever. Anybody will tell you that. Suppose you give somebody a dollar and they turn away, grumbling about how it's only a dollar. Do you give them another dollar? Or a hundred dollars? No! They're ungrateful, so you turn away. Do you think God is different?"

"Hatred is a destructive emotion that exhausts you. So avoid it. Whatever you hate, you attract that same thing to you. Whatever you fear, you attract to you. Whatever you love, you attract to you. Whatever you give, you attract to you. Whatever you focus on with strong emotions, you attract to you.

"You want to get rid of something in your life? Ignore it. I don't say ignore warning signs in your health. I'm saying ignore negative people. Ignore bad things. They'll go away. Focus on the opposite."

"Remember, everything is constantly changing. It's being created, changed, and destroyed, then given re-birth in some other form. This is nature. This is social progress. This is life. You're not the same person as you were yesterday. So get comfortable with that. Embrace it."

"People want a career path that goes in a straight line and upward without dips or diversions. Life's not like that. It may look like that if you're reading some-body's biography, but life is not linear; it's cyclical and expansive in all directions. Expand, expand, expand. Discard what's no longer of any use. And I mean that as personal beliefs or habits.

"If you make a commitment to someone, you can't discard that. You have to honor it. Americans say, 'Oh, I've changed and so we have to get a divorce.' No, you change, you have to learn to have a new relationship with your spouse. Because guess what: they've changed, too. So every day it's a new marriage, a new friendship, a new role as a parent. When your parents age, you get a new role as a child. You get to take care of them. Then they make you as crazy as you made them when you were a teenager (laughs)."

"You'll hear swamis talk about the Nature of Reality, and you'll think you know what they're talking about. 'Yes, this is reality, what we're all experiencing here right now', as opposed to what people using drugs or mentally unstable people are experiencing, which is not reality. But that's not it.

"The Nature of Reality is this: that whatever is going on inside of you is what's going on outside of you. And that particular reality is fluid. If things seem like they're not changing for the better, you're not changing for the better. You're still feeling and thinking and acting the same way, so your world is the same."

"The best advice I can give on this is this: look at the characteristics of the universe and try to match up with them. The universe is the biggest expression of love, so be the biggest expression of love. The universe is always creating, so be always creating whether you're working, playing, dreaming, with your friends, or meditating, or whatever.

"The universe doesn't keep score because the game is eternal. It just plays for the joy of playing. Be of service. Be generous. Don't look to advertising or celebrities for direction. Everything you need, you have."

## Things Mahesh Wants You to Remember

❀ There are universal laws. Know them or they will crush you.

- Everything is in motion.

- Security is an illusion.

- Everything in the universe is taken care of. You will be taken care of.

- The universe is law. The universe is personal. The universe is emotional. The universe is intelligent.

- One little touch into the substance of the divine, and a world is created. So your hopes, dreams, and aspirations for wealth and well-being seem big to you, but are small to it.

- Still, it will attend to your wants and needs with effortless and abundant compassion, delivering its bounty in wholly original and surprising ways. Just be open to its perfection that often resides outside our best laid plans.

- God is everywhere, all the time, ready to bless you beyond your wildest dreams. Allow Him to do so.